BEGINNING
TEACHERS'
LEARNING

Critical Guides for
Teacher Educators

You might also like the following books from Critical Publishing.

Developing Creative and Critical Educational Practitioners
Victoria Door
978-1-909682-37-5 Published 2014

Developing Outstanding Practice in School-based Teacher Education
Edited by Kim Jones and Elizabeth White
978-1-909682-41-2 Published 2014

Dial M for Mentor: Critical Reflections on Mentoring for Coaches, Educators and Trainers
Jonathan Gravells and Susan Wallace
978-1-909330-00-9 Published 2012

How do Expert Primary Classteachers Really Work? A Critical guide for Teachers, Headteachers and Teacher Educators
Tony Eaude
978-1-909330-01-6 Published 2012

Non-directive Coaching: Attitudes, Approaches and Applications
Bob Thomson
978-1-909330-57-3 Published 2013

Theories of Professional Learning
Carey Philpott
978-1-909682-33-7 Published 2014

Most of our titles are also available in a range of electronic formats. To order please go to our website www.criticalpublishing.com or contact our distributor, NBN International, 10 Thornbury Road, Plymouth PL6 7PP, telephone 01752 202301 or email orders@nbninternational.com.

BEGINNING
TEACHERS'
LEARNING

Making experience count

Series Editor: Ian Menter

Critical Guides for
Teacher Educators

Katharine **Burn**
Hazel **Hagger**
Trevor **Mutton**

First published in 2015 by Critical Publishing Ltd

British Library Cataloguing in Publication Data
A CIP record for this book is available from the British Library

ISBN: 978-1-910391-17-4

This book is also available in the following e-book formats:

MOBI: 978-1-910391-18-1
EPUB: 978-1-910391-19-8
Adobe e-book reader: 978-1-910391-20-4

The rights of Katharine Burn, Hazel Hagger and Trevor Mutton to be
identified as the Authors of this work have been asserted by them
in accordance with the Copyright, Design and Patents Act 1988.

Cover and text design by Greensplash Limited
Project Management by Out of House Publishing
Printed and bound in Great Britain by TJ International

Critical Publishing
152 Chester Road
Northwich
CW8 4AL

www.criticalpublishing.com

CONTENTS

Ian Menter is Professor of Teacher Education and Director of Professional Programmes in the Department of Education at the University of Oxford. He previously worked at the Universities of Glasgow, the West of Scotland, London Metropolitan, the West of England and Gloucestershire. Before that he was a primary school teacher in Bristol, England. His most recent publications include *A Literature Review on Teacher Education for the 21st Century* (Scottish Government) and *A Guide to Practitioner Research in Education* (Sage). His work has also been published in many academic journals.

Katharine Burn is an associate professor of education at the University of Oxford where she leads the PGCE history programme. She taught history for ten years in school and became fascinated by the process of professional learning, first as a mentor of beginning teachers and then as head of department. After completing a doctorate studying history teachers' learning in school and university, she became research officer for the Developing Expertise of Beginning Teachers (DEBT) project, a longitudinal study of 24 beginning teachers that traced their development over the course of their initial training and through the first two years of their careers.

Hazel Hagger was co-director of the DEBT project. She worked in secondary schools for many years before joining the University of Oxford in order to contribute to the development of one of the earliest initial teacher education (ITE) partnerships, and went on to become Director of Professional Programmes. Her doctoral research focused on ways of making practising teachers' expertise accessible to beginners and she has written extensively on teachers' learning and development.

Trevor Mutton is the current PGCE course director at the University of Oxford, where he also contributes to the Master's programme in learning and teaching. He taught modern foreign languages before joining the university and has since been involved in a range of research into language teaching and into the nature of beginning teachers' learning, including the DEBT project.

FOREWORD

It has become something of a cliché to say that those of us involved in teacher education *'live in interesting times'*. However, such has been the rate of change in many aspects of teacher education in many parts of the world over recent years, that this does actually need to be recognised. Because of the global interest in the quality of teaching and the recognition that teacher learning and the development of teachers play a crucial part in this, politicians and policymakers have shown increasing interest in the nature of teacher preparation. Early in 2013 the British Educational Research Association (BERA) in collaboration with the Royal Society for the Arts (RSA) established an inquiry into the relationship between research and teacher education. The final report from this inquiry was published in 2014 (BERA-RSA, 2014) and sets out a range of findings that include a call for all of those involved – policymakers, practitioners, researchers – *'to exercise leadership amongst their members and partners in promoting the use of evidence, enquiry and evaluation to prioritise the role of research and to make time and resources available for research engagement'* (p 27). One key purpose of this series of *Critical Guides for Teacher Educators* is to provide a resource that will facilitate a concerted move in this direction. The series aims to offer insights for all those with responsibilities in our field to support their critical engagement with practice and policy, through the use of evidence based on research and on experience.

This particular volume exemplifies this approach very clearly. The three authors, Katharine Burn, Hazel Hagger and Trevor Mutton, have been carrying out research together for several years now, largely based at Oxford University's Department of Education. Their collaborative project, entitled the Developing Expertise of Beginning Teachers (DEBT), has been distinctive in at least two respects. The first is that it has a strong longitudinal element and has thus been following beginning teachers from their initial teacher education into their first teaching posts. The second is that it really has examined closely the nature of experience in teacher learning and development. From their earlier collaborations with the much missed Donald McIntyre (eg, Hagger and McIntyre, 2006) through to their recent contribution to the BERA-RSA inquiry (Burn and Mutton, 2014), they have helped us to understand the relationship between theory and practice, and in particular to get to grips with the concept of *'clinical practice'* in teacher education. Although they are much published already, this is the first time that the collaborative work of the three of them has been drawn together in a book and I know that this will be an enormously helpful contribution in the development of high quality teacher education, wherever it is read.

Ian Menter, Series Editor

Professor of Teacher Education, University of Oxford

References

BERA-RSA (2014) *Research and the Teaching Profession – Building Capacity for a Self-Improving Education System.* London: BERA (available at bera.ac.uk).

Burn, K and Mutton, T (2014) *Review of 'Research-informed Clinical Practice' in Initial Teacher Education.* London: BERA (available at bera.ac.uk).

Hagger, H and McIntyre, D (2006) *Learning Teaching from Teachers: Realizing the Potential of School-based Teacher Education.* Maidenhead: Open University Press.

The ideal beginner

It is easy to paint a portrait of the ideal beginning teacher, to conjure up the mix of enthusiasm, thoughtfulness and commitment that characterises an effective learner and nascent colleague – someone with whom you would be happy to share your classes, to observe and advise as they get to grips with the demands of the role.

Such a trainee would arrive not only full of high aspirations for their pupils but also fully aware of how much they, too, had to learn. They would recognise the importance of thorough planning before any lesson and the value of finding out about their pupils' current levels of knowledge and common misconceptions before determining what their objectives should be. While they would seek advice at the planning stage and feedback on their early teaching endeavours, they would also take responsibility for self-evaluation and approach any debriefing with a list of aspects that they had already identified as requiring improvement and even some suggestions about how to make those changes.

While aware of their weaknesses, they would take a realistic view of their own development, recognising where things had genuinely worked well and seeking to build on them. They would welcome constructive criticism, accepting it in the positive spirit in which it was intended, and look for opportunities to take it on board. They would also be alert to the opportunities available to them to learn from their pupils: identifying from the pupils' difficulties where a fuller explanation was needed; paying attention to the pupils' questions and the strategies on which they tended to rely, in order to rethink their own instruction and consider alternative methods.

This may all sound too good to be true, but this particular portrait is not an imaginary one. Although we have given him a pseudonym, Hanif, whom we tracked within a research project through his training year and on into his first two years as a qualified mathematics teacher, displayed all these qualities. He was indeed an outstanding trainee who made tremendous progress. His mentor and other colleagues within the mathematics department thoroughly enjoyed working with him and were always happy to share their ideas, advice and resources with him (as they did with each other). Moreover, the approaches that he had adopted as a trainee continued to inspire his professional learning over the next two years. He always recognised that there was more to learn, insisting that every lesson brought something new. When invited to predict how his first year as a newly qualified teacher (NQT) might compare with his training year, he immediately emphasised his need to go on learning:

Well, for a start the big similarity is that I'll always be learning. Even going beyond an NQT, there is always going to be something else that I can learn. So many million more things that I can learn, in fact.

He was adamant that if the day came when he failed to learn anything new, he would leave teaching.

This positive approach, established during his training year, was undoubtedly helped by an exemplary induction mentor, who set aside regular meeting times each week during Hanif's first year of teaching. This mentor went further, ensuring that the following year's timetable would allow them to keep teaching parallel classes, thus enabling them to compare strategies and collaborate closely in developing schemes of work. While Hanif took full advantage of his colleague's support, he also continued to recognise how much his pupils had to teach him:

The 30 kids: they're just as good as an observer sitting at the back of the room watching what's going on. Their experience enables them to comment, and that's another piece of the mosaic that can be put in to make the fuller picture.

Where Hanif had relied initially on rigorous planning, he became more alert to the range of ways in which pupils might respond to particular ideas and therefore of the need to establish a clear framework for the lesson within which he could be increasingly responsive to their learning. He repeatedly referred to his marking as an opportunity to reflect on his teaching and frequently sought advice from his classes about the effectiveness of strategies he had used. He also took on certain kinds of responsibility, such as that of IT co-ordinator within the department, that would allow him to talk to colleagues about exactly how they used particular equipment, such as interactive whiteboards and graphic calculators, in their teaching. It is hardly surprising that the adjective we chose to sum up Hanif's teaching career at the end of his second year was *'flourishing'!*

Case studies of more complex trajectories

But not everyone is like Hanif. Far from it. While most trainees display many positive dispositions, some of their assumptions about how they will learn to teach and some of their previous experiences may make it much more difficult for them to engage effectively in the processes of school-based training. Moreover, even those who begin professional training with dispositions similar to those displayed by Hanif can become frustrated or overwhelmed if their introduction to the challenges of teaching is inappropriately supported or proves too abrupt or complex for them to handle. Brilliant graduates with equally high aspirations for their pupils may find their early failures hard to bear and struggle to make sense of, or to connect with, their pupils' current perspectives. Career changers, highly skilled in other fields, may struggle to come to terms with their novice status and their lack of the knowledge and skills that experienced teachers take for granted. Passionate but inexperienced novices, desperate to prove themselves in challenging contexts, may misinterpret advice as personal criticism or quickly lose confidence if that advice does not seem to be immediately effective.

In offering guidance to school-based teacher educators, as this book seeks to do, it makes sense not to focus on the stars who are obviously following a brilliant trajectory, but to concentrate on those beginners with more complicated journeys, teasing out from their experiences the nature of the difficulties that learning to teach can present, before identifying those mentoring strategies that do most to generate and sustain a positive orientation towards learning from experience in school. The three case studies that follow are therefore intended to establish the key challenges and questions that this book addresses. All of them are teachers that we encountered, like Hanif, in our three-year research project studying the Developing Expertise of Beginning Teachers (the DEBT project). (See, for example, Hagger et al, 2008; Mutton et al, 2010; Burn et al, 2010.)

The DEBT project

Altogether we tracked 24 teachers for three years, recruiting them from two well-established partnership schemes at the beginning of their training year. In each case, their Postgraduate Certificate in Education (PGCE) programme was planned jointly by the university and participating schools, and included 120 days spent in school, divided between two placements. The data that we collected included observation (and filming) of individual lessons taught at regular intervals – four times during the PGCE year, and once a term for the following two years. This gave us ten lessons for each teacher, each followed by an interview, in which we asked the teacher to break the lesson into its main sections and first to describe and then to evaluate each section in whatever way they chose. We probed their responses, inviting them to share any thoughts about possible refinements or adaptations in light of their reflections, but not offering any judgements or suggestions of our own. We also asked them to explain the thinking behind their planning and to reflect at the end on any particular insights that they had gained from it. Once we had finished discussing the lesson, we asked them to reflect in more general terms on their professional learning since we had last seen them. At the end of each year we invited them to review their development over the whole period.

In collecting and analysing this data, we were guided by two central research questions: 'What are the beginning teachers learning?' and 'How are they learning?'. In the case studies that follow we are mainly drawing on our findings about how the teachers were learning – particularly their approach towards learning from experience, which was obviously fundamental to their learning in school, both during the PGCE year and as they took up their first professional post. We will draw on this analysis in more detail in subsequent chapters, but here we present their stories to help you think about the challenges involved in learning to teach and their implications for anyone trying to support that learning in school.

Case Study 1
Limiting the vision to reduce the challenge: Rhiannon

Rhiannon, like Hanif, was a mathematics trainee. Although she had not previously worked in schools, experience leading a lively Brownie pack had given her a good grounding in managing groups of young people, and an awareness of the importance of effective organisation and clear instructions when setting up tasks. She was therefore quite well prepared for her early lessons and actually found it easier than Hanif had done to arrive appropriately prepared with resources ready as she needed them. However, while she clearly found mathematics interesting and enjoyable, she rarely communicated the same enthusiasm as he did or became as caught up in thinking about how the pupils were trying to make sense of the ideas that they were working with. While Hanif was always alert to pupils' thinking and increasingly tried to understand how they were interpreting new ideas, Rhiannon's focus on their learning was more narrowly directed towards ensuring that they had got things right. At least it *became* much more narrowly focused after one of her earliest lessons, when she had tried to adopt a much more open, discovery-oriented approach and had quickly become overwhelmed by the diversity of responses that this had yielded.

This particular lesson seemed to be profoundly influential in Rhiannon's early development. She had been encouraged to try out an exploratory activity, in which pupils could choose the collection of three numbers that they used in plotting a particular spiral pattern on squared paper. However, the pupils, who embraced the challenge quite enthusiastically, soon began to make more unusual choices that Rhiannon had not anticipated. These gave rise to more complicated variations, making it difficult for them to identify the recurring features and rules underlying the formation of particular patterns. Rhiannon's response, as she saw the path she had mapped out splintering into myriad different trails, was to close down the pupils' options, restricting the choices they could make so that the outcomes became easier for her to manage.

This unsettling experience, and Rhiannon's rather panicked reaction to it, seemed to freeze her development, making her much less ambitious in her choice of teaching strategies and essentially less ambitious for the pupils' learning. More significantly perhaps, the willingness that she had shown in that particular lesson to experiment with investigative approaches to mathematics education almost entirely disappeared thereafter. While she had previously been quite keen to try things out, she became much more reluctant to take risks to broaden her repertoire. The deliberate commitment to her own learning and capacity to plan for it, so evident in her approach to that particular lesson, effectively disappeared and did not reappear in our interviews with Rhiannon until the end of her NQT year.

This is not to say that Rhiannon did not go on to learn a great deal. In each interview during the training year, she could identify new insights from her teaching and commented positively on how much progress she had made. She also referred to a range of sources from which she was learning, including observation of other teachers, the opportunity to mark pupils' books and her mentor's feedback, which was *'helping the most'*. Her comments, however, were almost always focused on what she had already learned; we rarely heard her articulate any kind of agenda for her future learning. Her approach seemed to be essentially reactive: looking back, often with a degree of surprise and bewilderment, to discover what she had learned, rather than identifying specific issues that she intended to address.

I don't know really. It's strange. It's all just happening. It's not until I look back at the Standards and I think 'Gosh, I'm doing this! This is just happening naturally now.' I'm getting constant feedback from the other teachers, the other members of staff, and that's brilliant. They highlight things that I never think of, whether it's just because they are sitting at the back and just observing the whole lesson and they can pick up on particular things, whereas because I'm involved right in there within the class and in the teaching I'm not aware of certain things.

As this reflection reveals, Rhiannon found it difficult to focus her attention on specific aspects while she was teaching. In reporting her perceptions of particular lessons, her accounts were noticeably shorter than Hanif's and tended to be concerned with her management of the pupils and of the activities. There was much less explicit consideration of the pupils' thinking or of their approaches to particular kinds of question. In the early lesson discussed above, the pupils' diverse responses essentially presented themselves as a management problem. The only other occasions on which Rhiannon focused in detail on the pupils' capabilities and their approaches to mathematical problems tended to be when she was discussing tasks attempted for homework that she was marking later. These gave her the chance to think more carefully about their learning than was possible during lessons.

The feedback that Rhiannon valued so highly and her determination to create well-ordered and appropriately managed lessons undoubtedly gave her a secure grounding in teaching and a basic repertoire of strategies about which she could feel confident. However, there was little excitement or passion invested in her work, and lessons tended to follow a rather predictable format. The ideas on which she drew in explaining her plans came from a limited range of sources, essentially restricted to her placement school, but she showed little awareness that the pupils in her classes could also be a key resource in helping her to develop further.

While Rhiannon was able to consolidate her knowledge and skills as she settled into her first year of teaching, we saw few signs of significant development. Although she referred to her head of department as an invaluable source of support and guidance, she rarely identified new priorities or particular issues that she wanted to address. Her frame of reference tended to remain limited to ideas within the scheme of work and the school's resources. Her learning was still largely undirected, arising particularly from identifying and responding to her own mistakes. Since fewer things were obviously going wrong, her learning curve had become *'much less steep'* than in her training year. However, it was clear that she felt well supported and was given considerable encouragement, feedback and a number of opportunities to learn from others.

Although Rhiannon's ambitions seemed to remain limited during her first year of teaching, the formal opportunities that she was given to observe other teachers were clearly bearing fruit during her second year, when a programme of shared observation and feedback was extended more systematically across the department. While she had remained nervous in her first year about pupils experimenting with different approaches to particular kinds of problems, her outlook seemed to undergo a gradual but striking change over the course of the following year. Not only did she talk more positively about investigative work and start advising the pupils to try out different ways of approaching particular questions or tasks, she also began to recognise that the pupils could be a key resource for her learning as a teacher and that she needed to pay attention to what they could offer:

It's the feedback from the pupils that's surprising me and affecting the way that I teach or that I think about teaching. If I think I know a class and I know the individuals, the pitch of the lesson is always directed at them, suited for their level. But if the pupils are still going to surprise me about their level and their understanding, then I'm still going to have to alter the pitch and the level each time.

While this uncertainty would previously have troubled her, she had, by the end of her second year, developed sufficient confidence to deviate from her plans and to respond much more directly to the pupils' particular needs:

I would guess that my confidence is probably reflected in my teaching, that I'm not as rigid in my lesson plans, in my lesson delivery. I've now got the confidence to be able to swap and change things more readily than I would have done before.

Questions raised by Rhiannon's experience

Rhiannon began with an ambitious and optimistic view of the scope for pupils to pursue their own lines of enquiry – to see mathematics, not as a body of knowledge arbitrarily defined by others, but as a set of patterns and principles that they could identify and begin to exploit for themselves. When she saw how difficult it could be to manage such an exploratory activity and realised that she was ill-equipped to respond to pupils' diverse questions, she quickly panicked and closed down their options to make the task easier to manage. This experience seemed to reduce her expectations of the pupils and ultimately to limit her aspirations for her own learning. The questions that her experience raises include the following.

>> How can school-based teacher educators set up early teaching tasks that are straightforward enough for trainees to manage, but that do not reduce genuinely complex – and potentially exciting – subjects to simplistic and reductive exercises?

>> How can we ensure that trainees' early teaching experiences are positive and successful ones that build their confidence without narrowing their vision of effective teaching?

>> How can we help trainee teachers to develop an accurate knowledge of pupils' current understandings and common misconceptions, without limiting and reducing their ambitions for their future learning?

While Rhiannon certainly used the range of sources that was made available to support her learning, she tended to rely heavily on the resources that others provided. Even as her ambitions were rekindled by her increasing confidence, she still depended on opportunities for learning created by others. It was a long time before she recognised how much she could learn from her pupils, by paying attention to their diverse ideas and ways of working rather than simply trying to channel their thinking into pre-determined pathways. So the following questions arise.

» How can we ensure that the structured programmes that we put in place provide appropriate stimulus and guidance for trainees' learning, without making trainees so dependent on that provision that they do not adopt more productive approaches to their own learning?

» How can we equip trainees to learn effectively from the resource to which they will always have the greatest access and that can tell them most about the effectiveness of their teaching strategies: the pupils in their classrooms?

Case Study 2
Desperate to prove herself and devastated by 'failure': Anita

Anita's development, throughout her training year and beyond, was similarly shaped by some of her earliest difficulties. Their impact in her case was not to restrict her vision but to paralyse her emotionally. While she retained her own strong vision of effective teaching, her early failures left her determined to prove her competence to herself and to others, but in many respects unwilling or unable to map out the steps by which she might reach that point.

The greatest challenge that Anita faced was the fact that she had already been a successful and highly respected health-care professional, entrusted with significant responsibilities in emergency care and well used to advising junior colleagues in training. The experience of starting again in a new profession and admitting just how much she had to learn proved far more difficult than she had expected. While she formally acknowledged the idea of going back to the beginning, being robbed of her status as a skilled professional made her extremely vulnerable and prone to despair.

The sense of professional responsibility that she carried, previously for her patients and now for pupils, meant that Anita found 'mistakes' very difficult to deal with. While she expressed a positive commitment to learning effectively from them, the sense that she had let someone down was difficult to bear. As she told us, a few months into her training year:

I never make the same mistake twice, because of where I've come from. I've left something that I was very good at and I've left something with a great deal of responsibility. It does hurt that I'm beginning again… but with each mistake I make, I really do ponder on it and it does wear me out, and it does have an effect. At least I know that I've dealt with that and it won't come up again.

While 'pondering' one's mistakes sounds like an appropriate thing to do – and was indeed one source of Hanif's rapid development – Anita took them so much to heart that she found it virtually impossible to separate criticism of her teaching from criticism of herself. Indeed, so frustrated was she by her own inability to achieve what she wanted in the first few months, that she even tended to reject praise and encouragement for other features of her practice as essentially unhelpful and undeserved. Feedback on one of her earliest lessons, which had included quite a detailed focus on organisational and instructional aspects as she tried to manage a series of group tasks, reduced her to tears despite its positive aspects:

The other feedback was very constructive, but I felt destroyed by it because I thought 'I am not this person'. The positive things were just so weak. ... That's why I thought 'Nice, but dim. Here comes this teacher who doesn't know what she's doing; but she's friendly and won't shout at us.' I don't want to be like that. I'm not ashamed to tell you that I feel awful. I don't want to go there. I feel like this child. I feel very vulnerable.

The sense of *'failure'* in Anita's case was compounded by the fact that she was one of two trainee English teachers in the same department, and she felt that her own practice was continually being compared unfavourably with that of the other beginner. This was not necessarily the case, but the assumption that it was exerted a powerful influence, magnifying Anita's sense of inadequacy and the shock of realising that she was no longer seen as a highly competent professional.

Anita was desperate to regain that status and the respect that went with it, and did indeed make good progress in mastering specific techniques, enabling her, for example, to manage group tasks effectively and to give clear instructions. However, there were few signs of her actually setting out the priorities for her development and mapping the steps by which she might achieve them. She undoubtedly had strong views about what she would like her pupils to achieve and how she would like them to work, but these were never clearly articulated. Her desire to reach the point where she would be recognised as a good teacher effectively became a source of frustration, rather than serving as a guide to the journey that she needed to make.

The lack of planning for her own learning may also have reflected the nature of Anita's aspirations for her pupils. These tended to be expressed in terms of the quality of relationships within her classroom and the ways in which the pupils would approach their work, rather than as more specific objectives framed as knowledge or understanding of the subject. Anita's vision of learning English was strongly shaped by a commitment to creativity and a concern to capture pupils' imagination, which seemed to militate against a high degree of forward planning. A similar attitude was echoed in reflections on how her practice might develop, simply conceding that *'I'm not a list person. I think it will come with experience'*. While she could later look back and identify the steps that she had made, there were few examples of her looking forward and suggesting specific aspects of her practice on which she intended to focus.

None of this is to suggest that Anita did not work hard. She cared passionately about the pupils' experience and invested considerable time in designing resources; but the very fact that she invested so much often made her more prone to frustration or despair. Moreover, partly as a result of her commitment to creativity, and perhaps partly inspired by her belief that as a trained professional she *ought* to be able to do this job, Anita often found herself pulling in different directions from her mentor and other class teachers. At times, this meant that she developed her own procedures, rejecting, for example, the school's system of yellow and red cards used to warn pupils about unacceptable behaviour and devising her own methods instead. At other times, it became a source of resentment and of blame if things did not go well. The conflict was most obvious late in the year when she was asked to begin a study of *'poems from other cultures'* with a Year 9 class that had just completed a number of formal assessment tasks. Anita's conviction that the children deserved a break and the chance to engage in more creative, or at least more accessible, work meant that she was ill-disposed to accept advice or to explore how the actual lessons could have been made more engaging. In her eyes, the difficulties that the pupils experienced were only to be expected given what had been asked of her. Her assumption was that she bore no responsibility for the problems that arose and could not reasonably be expected to consider alternative approaches to achieving the lesson objectives.

Despite these frustrations during her training year, Anita's dedication, hard work and wealth of subject knowledge enabled her to demonstrate the full range of competences required, and within her first two years of teaching she went on to achieve some of her particular ambitions, including the design and in-house publication of a collection of pupils' creative writing, which was very well received. Her qualities were recognised and valued by certain colleagues who later encouraged her to seek specific promotions. However, her position always seemed to be an embattled one, in which she defined her own approaches in opposition to other people, at times claiming the pupils as her allies against the system.

Anita's approach to her own learning over the next two years followed a remarkably similar pattern to that of her training year. While she would express a range of objectives for her own learning, these were never accompanied by specific strategies to address them, and by the end of both her first and second year, the overwhelming sense was one of exhaustion, preventing her from learning anything new. She was frequently resistant to advice, appealing instead to her own convictions and ideals. She often felt resentful that her efforts were not more widely appreciated, sometimes criticising the systems within which she was constrained to operate for promoting control and order rather than learning, and sometimes resentful of the pupils for their failure to reciprocate the hard work which she invested in supporting them. Her progress, and certainly her own sense of her development, were thus highly chequered and seemed, at times, very fragile indeed. While she craved reassurance and support, the strength – and simultaneous lack of clarity – of some of her convictions, combined with her enduring assumption that she really ought to be able to do this by herself, made it very difficult for those who tried to support her professional learning.

Questions raised by Anita's experience

The nature of Anita's difficulties reveals three distinct, but overlapping, issues of which school-based teacher educators, and especially those working with career changers, need to be aware. The first is the need for trainees to embrace an identity as a learner, even while striving for acceptance and affirmation of their identity as a teacher. For those who have already achieved recognition in one professional field, the status of novice can be particularly hard to bear. But such tensions are not confined to those who have lost the credibility they had once earned. The desire to be seen as competent, which is magnified in a system in which mentors act not just as guides but as assessors, can make any beginner so anxious to demonstrate how well they can *perform* that they fail to focus effectively on what they actually need to learn.

The second issue is the tension between valuing creativity (as an approach to – and outcome of – learning) and respecting the structures and organisational processes necessary for monitoring and sustaining learning in a school context. Anita's view of what it meant to learn English equipped her with very powerful ambitions for her pupils' learning, but she struggled to articulate and plan the specific steps by which she might enable them to achieve those heights. The lack of structure and precision in her thinking made it difficult to chart her progress towards those goals and made her particularly prone to feelings of failure.

Anita's frustration was compounded by a third issue: her tendency to interpret constructive criticism of her teaching as personal criticism of her. Because effective teaching depends on establishing secure and productive relationships with the learners, trainees can find it extremely difficult to separate their teaching role from their personal identity. Since she had lost her former professional identity, Anita's experience of this problem was particularly acute, but she is far from unique in interpreting others' judgements of her teaching as personal judgements of her.

Consideration of these three challenges and of the ways in which they interact raises a further series of questions for school-based teacher educators.

> » How can we encourage trainees to embrace the idea of being seen as a learner, rather than viewing such an identity as a transitional one that they are seeking to shed as soon as possible?

> » How can we properly acknowledge the diverse knowledge, skills and expertise that trainees may have acquired in previous careers or other roles, and capitalise on their obvious success as learners in those different contexts?

> » How can we help trainees to understand and work effectively within the structures and policies that operate in our particular school, while retaining a critical perspective that will enable them to contribute to their evaluation and perhaps subsequent improvement?

> » How can we help trainees to think critically and constructively about their ambitions for pupils' learning, turning worthwhile but undefined aspirations into specific developmental steps (for them as teachers, as well as for the pupils)?

» How can we provide feedback that focuses trainees' attention not on themselves but on their pupils' learning?

» How can we acknowledge the personal dimension in teaching, making us appropriately sensitive in providing feedback and able to present it in ways that focus trainees' attention not on themselves but on their pupils' learning?

Case Study 3
Early competence but restricted growth: Rob

Rob's early teaching was much more obviously successful than Anita's, and in his case, this success was directly attributable to his prior experience: two years' voluntary work, teaching science in West Africa. Unfortunately, the advantages which this previous work gave him and the relative ease and speed with which he demonstrated his competence as a teacher may, when combined with rather poorly focused mentoring, actually have restricted the scope for his subsequent development.

Rob certainly believed that his previous teaching experience shaped his approach to the opportunities for learning within his training programme. He had become used to coping with large classes, minimal resources and highly unpredictable support structures, which made him very self-reliant. Superficially, his aspirations appeared very high. Like Hanif, he often declared that there was always more to learn about teaching. Yet his declaration that learning to teach was *'a never-ending tunnel'* with *'no Holy Grail'* ever to be attained actually translated into a pragmatic acceptance that there was no point in even striving to reach it. His vague aspirations thus never became specific plans for addressing particular challenges and his approach to his own learning was never a very active one. As he admitted near the end of his first year, *'I'm not learning through a conscious effort – just through experience, which may or may not be useful for the future'*. The standard by which he judged his performance was essentially a gut reaction, not really focused on the pupils' learning, but on whether or not he *'felt comfortable'* with it.

The sources of ideas on which Rob drew became narrower as his training year went on. While he referred in early interviews to insights and suggestions explored in university seminars, such as the need to capture pupils' curiosity with good visual hooks and the value of encouraging pupils to make predictions about the outcome of experiments as a way of eliciting and subsequently challenging their current conceptual understanding, he became increasingly reliant on the suggestions within his school's schemes of work. On only one occasion did he refer to seeking advice from his university tutor, asking about ways of dealing with a particularly noisy class. As a result of adopting some of the tutor's suggestions and finding that they *'worked'* for some pupils but not for others, Rob concluded that every teaching situation is unique, so there is little to be gained from research-based insights. He felt that he could only go on *'plugging away'*, learning more about each highly specific situation – learning which, by its nature, could not be transferred to other situations. In discussing particular challenges or difficulties, he tended to attribute them to his lack of knowledge of a specific activity or of the precise subject content, or to the relatively short time he had had to build a rapport with pupils. They would be solved, he assumed, simply by gaining more experience.

That experience, combined with the confidence and practical skills that he had already mastered, enabled Rob to demonstrate many of the teaching standards with relative ease, prompting his mentor to withdraw much of his support and guidance. By the time of our second interview, early in the spring term, Rob was receiving very little feedback. This was something that he appeared to regret, although at no point did he ever actually ask for more frequent observation or more extensive analysis of his lessons.

I had a mentor session yesterday in which he said something about – he doesn't see the need to observe many of my lessons… He basically said to me, 'You're competent enough. We want you to work here next year.' Which basically misses the point in that I'm supposed to be learning. I'm supposed to be getting more feedback, but I'm not. It's a problem in a way. If I'm unsure about something, I can obviously ask, but I'm not getting the voluntary response. Maybe there is a problem in my teaching that I don't know about and I'm not seeing.

While Rob's reaction hinted at a desire to be pushed further – an aspiration that could perhaps have been cultivated – the fact that he took no positive steps to request the observation and feedback to which he was entitled, nor sought out alternative resources, suggested an essentially reactive, rather than a proactive, orientation towards his own learning. He never subsequently referred (as Hanif invariably did) to what he could learn from the pupils by attending to their questions and ways of working, although he did value the insights that were presented to him in other ways. He frequently commented, for example, that our interview questions, prompting him to describe and reflect on each lesson that we observed, helped him to identify and evaluate issues that he had not previously considered. Yet his lack of initiative in seeking similar opportunities or constructing deliberate plans to develop his practice essentially suggested that he was ill-equipped to go on learning beyond his training year and might well remain satisfied with an essentially competent performance.

In his first year of teaching there were some indications that Rob might prove us wrong. He did, for example, actively seek advice from experienced heads of department within the local area when he found himself without a subject leader in his own school, and he took the decision to attend a course on curriculum and management organised by the Royal Society of Chemistry. In planning to take on a new A-level syllabus, he set up some experimental sessions with Year 12 pupils to test out their reactions to its particular emphases. But these signs of initiative in relation to his learning all tended to be focused on curriculum choice and administrative responsibilities rather than on classroom teaching. There was little evidence that he sought to broaden his frame of reference in similar ways when thinking about pedagogy. The challenges that he faced – those of motivating pupils and managing their behaviour, and of organising his time effectively to ensure that he could get work marked and returned to them – were all tackled through trial and error. Once he felt that they had been overcome, he showed little awareness of learning anything new in relation to classroom teaching and saw progressively little value in the sessions provided locally for NQTs.

With a few, rare exceptions, Rob's interview responses continued to suggest a lack of aspiration for pupil learning, and his focus appeared simply to be on what he needed to do to function effectively. His reflections were rooted in the practical requirements of the tasks and responsibilities that he faced and when asked about his own learning, his answers became increasingly succinct, suggesting a degree of impatience with the idea of continued professional learning.

This sense of reluctance or difficulty in answering questions about his learning persisted during Rob's second year of teaching, when he attributed the problem to a lack of time for reflection. Indeed, lack of time was a persistent theme and in response to those pressures, he consciously adopted a *'good enough'* philosophy to lesson preparation, claiming that the school's existing resources were actually quite good and that *'if it works there's no point changing it'*. He readily admitted that his ambitions for improving pupils' learning experiences were deliberately limited as a means of coping with the range of pressures on his time.

While he attributed most improvements in his practice simply to the fact that his classes were more familiar with him, he did continue to experiment and try out ideas in a relatively informal way as a means of developing highly specific new skills (eg, extending his use of IT to include data logging equipment by *'playing around with it myself, and seeing what it can do'*). When facing certain sorts of challenges or new responsibilities, Rob clearly could take a deliberative approach to his own learning, but looking back over the course of two years, he felt that his learning had been essentially unplanned – something of which he was barely conscious: *'it has tended to be a gradual process – you change very slowly – I think it's probably more obvious to those who are looking in from outside'*. As he looked ahead to new challenges, he anticipated the continued use of a *'trial and error approach'*, expecting, for example, that his work now acting as mentor to a newly qualified teacher would be *'a bit hit and miss'*.

Questions raised by Rob's experience

Rob's development obviously has many positive features. But his own awareness that he was not being guided as effectively as he could have been, and his tendency to settle for what appeared to be working, suggests that with encouragement to engage in more systematic evaluation of pupils' learning, he might have made much more significant progress. Given the strength of his organisational skills and practical knowledge, he could have paid more attention within lessons to the pupils' developing understanding, rather than simply reviewing whether the practical tasks had been carried out successfully. Given his capacity to take action when he saw a development need – as he did in relation to the introduction of new A-level specifications – it was disappointing not to see him sustain a similarly proactive and systematic approach to aspects of classroom teaching, such as developing the quality of his explanations or refining his use of questions.

The questions raised by Rob's case echo some of those that we identified in thinking about Rhiannon. While her initial aspirations were reduced when she realised the practical challenges that they entailed, Rob's ambitions were much more limited from the start; but in both cases it was unsurprising that their lack of vision also tended to mean a lack of planning for their own learning. Further questions raised by his story include the following.

» How can we ensure that trainees go on learning throughout their training year and beyond, rather than settling into a comfortable routine once they feel they have mastered the basics?

» How can we ensure that the range of sources on which beginning teachers draw, both in planning their teaching and in reviewing its effectiveness, extend beyond the resources available to them within their particular school context?

» How can we help trainees to identify the strategies that they are employing in relation to other aspects of their professional learning (such as subject knowledge development or familiarisation with particular exam specifications) and apply them in the development of their classroom teaching?

Key questions addressed by this book

In reviewing the questions generated by each case study, and contrasting the more uneven journeys with Hanif's glowing trajectory, it becomes clear that the important issues that we need to consider in supporting trainees' learning in school derive as much from the nature of teaching itself as they do from the way in which beginners approach the whole process of learning to be a teacher.

If we are to support beginners effectively, we first need to acknowledge just how complex the task of teaching is. If we do not adequately recognise the challenges involved in planning and structuring sequences of learning activities for up to 30 individuals, in devising and targeting questions, and framing effective feedback to their varied responses, then we will fail to prepare our trainees for the shock of that discovery. Only by taking proper account of the range of challenges that teaching presents can we work out how to structure and sequence trainees' engagement with those challenges in ways that neither overwhelm them nor leave them satisfied with simple solutions. And only by acknowledging how much there is to be learned and that the process is necessarily an ongoing one – indeed, that it is a career-long professional commitment – can we find ways of reconciling the tensions inherent in assuming an identity as a teacher while continuing to see oneself as a learner. Chapter 2 therefore asks 'What are the challenges involved in learning to teach?'

Once we have understood the task in which they are engaged, we can turn our attention to the trainees themselves. As four cases have already illustrated, there is no such thing as a *typical* trainee. Each individual is shaped not only by their own experiences and expectations of formal education but also by other roles that they have played, within families and in different work contexts. The different approaches that they adopt are also determined by their assumptions about the process of learning to teach, particularly their understanding of what it means to learn from experience. Building on what we have already established about the differences between beginning teachers in terms of their starting points and the trajectories that they pursue, Chapter 3 asks *What do we know about beginning teachers as learners?* identifying the most important kinds of difference between them and highlighting the kind of dispositions towards learning that seem to be of most use to them.

After considering the challenges involved in the process and what we know about beginning teachers' approaches to those challenges, we will be equipped to answer the most important question of all: *'How can we help beginning teachers to become more effective learners?'* Chapter 4 is therefore devoted to presenting and exemplifying a series of principles that school-based teacher educators can use to guide their practice.

In answering each set of questions we will draw not only on the DEBT project and our many years' experience working with beginning teachers, but also on the wealth of wider research into school-based teacher education. This research was first stimulated in England by the establishment of teacher education partnerships in the early 1990s and has been given fresh impetus by the international *'practicum turn'* (Mattson et al, 2011) in teacher education. There is now a rich variety on which to draw. Quantitative and qualitative research methods have served to illuminate both the range and the nature of beginning teachers' experiences, while our perspective is enriched by combining the insights from academic researchers with those of school-based teacher educators using action research approaches to deepen their understanding of the needs of their trainees and to evaluate and refine their mentoring skills.

IN A **NUTSHELL**

Just four case studies serve to demonstrate the dangers inherent in thinking about a *typical trainee*. The differences between beginning teachers derive not just from their diverse prior experiences (within and beyond the worlds of education) and contrasting conceptions of effective learning within particular subjects, but also from their assorted assumptions about the learning process itself and the particular positions that they adopt in seeking to reconcile the dual role required of them as learner and teacher. The challenges for those seeking to guide and direct any particular beginner are compounded by the fact that teaching itself is a complex, multi-faceted task. While ways have to be found of simplifying that complexity in order to nurture beginners' confidence and furnish them with some secure footholds, effective development depends ultimately on equipping beginners to learn effectively in the context of real classrooms. As school-based educators, we can only equip them to do so by paying close attention first to the nature of teaching and the processes involved in learning to teach, and then to the key characteristics of trainees and their dispositions towards learning from experience.

CRITICAL ISSUES **TO BE ADDRESSED**

- *What are the challenges of learning to teach? (Chapter 2)*
- *What do we know about beginning teachers as learners? (Chapter 3)*
- *How can we help beginning teachers to become more effective learners? (Chapter 4)*

CHAPTER 2 | WHAT ARE THE CHALLENGES OF LEARNING TO TEACH?

CRITICAL **ISSUES**

- *What are the different kinds of knowledge that teachers need?*
- *Why can teaching not be reduced to a clear set of prescriptions to follow?*
- *What makes learning to teach so different from other kinds of learning?*
- *What tensions do beginners face in combining the roles of teacher and learner?*

The complexity of teaching

This book began with a case study of a highly successful beginning teacher, Hanif. We illustrated his passionate commitment to his own learning by quoting a prediction he made at the end of his training year – a confident declaration that he would *always* be learning:

Even going beyond an NQT, there is always going to be something else that I can learn. So many million more things that I can learn, in fact.

The problem for teachers at the start of their training is that Hanif is basically right! Darling-Hammond (2006), who has worked with colleagues systematically mapping out the knowledge that teachers need, refers to the *'spectacular array'* of things that teachers should know and be able to do in their work. Although the framework of knowledge, skills and dispositions that they outline (Bransford et al, 2005) is structured in relation to three basic dimensions – knowledge of learners and learning; knowledge of subject matter and curriculum goals; and knowledge of teaching – the range of different aspects that each dimension encompasses and the complex interplay between them make the prospect of trying to get to grips with them all a formidable undertaking.

The range of knowledge that teachers need

1. Knowledge of learners and learning

Knowledge of how young people learn and develop, not as an individual process but within the social context of the classroom (with reference to the wider contexts of their families and communities), requires not only an understanding of general developmental progression but also of individual differences in learning. Given the range of pupils within many of our classrooms, beginning teachers need a much deeper knowledge base about teaching for diverse learners than ever before and more highly developed diagnostic abilities to guide their decisions. To build most effectively on what pupils already know, they also need to be aware of what young people have learnt during their early years and are continuing to learn outside school.

2. Knowledge of subject matter and curriculum goals

Teaching at any level requires a deep understanding of the subject content that is to be taught. Even in the case of graduates teaching their degree subject at secondary level, such knowledge cannot be taken for granted. Historians may, for example, have to teach periods with which they are unfamiliar; biologists will almost certainly have to teach physics. The range of subjects taught by primary teachers means that there will always be those about which they need to learn more. But, as Shulman and his colleagues at Stanford have powerfully argued, content knowledge is very different from curricular knowledge, or what they term *'pedagogical content knowledge'* (Shulman 1986, p 9) – a developed awareness of the underlying concepts and organisational structures within a particular subject domains, and of the most logical or effective sequences of steps by which knowledge may be built within them. Curricular knowledge encompasses not only clearly framed and well-justified goals and models of progression, but also familiarity with the kinds of misconceptions that often prevent pupils from developing more powerful ideas. Even where the curriculum itself has been specified in detail by national requirements or exam syllabuses, teachers need sufficiently secure knowledge to make a wide variety of curriculum decisions, ranging from the evaluation and selection of materials to the design and sequencing of tasks or assignments, based on pupils' current learning needs.

3. Knowledge of teaching

The teaching strategies most apparent to trainees are probably those concerned with explanation, instruction and questioning. As Bransford et al (2005, p 35) observe, the range of strategies that beginners need to master are concerned with the processes of *'motivating and organizing students'* work in settings that provide access to challenging content and frequent assessments of their progress, coupled with feedback and opportunities to revise and improve. Classroom management is obviously of fundamental importance, but it extends far beyond rules for classroom conduct and procedures to deal with misbehaviour, drawing, for example, on motivation theory and the management of groups in order to create a psychologically safe and productive learning environment. While beginners need to develop a repertoire of strategies that might be used in teaching any subject, they also need a storehouse of representations and analogies for teaching specific topics. And to judge their effectiveness, they need a similar range of formative assessment strategies – tools that will allow them to tap into pupils' current thinking and levels of understanding, alerting them to the need to adapt their teaching to the progress that those pupils are making. Formative assessment, of course, ultimately has to be connected to the demands of summative assessment. Beginners also need to know how to use locally defined standards or national assessment objectives to construct, mark and interpret the results of more formal assessments.

This complexity is easy for both you and your trainees to overlook. For you, as an experienced teacher, able to read a classroom fluently and to select from an extensive repertoire of well-tuned strategies, it can be all too easy to forget just how much you have learned over time, how many of your deliberate practices have now become routinised, and on how many different kinds of insight you are drawing. For a beginning teacher, habituated to classrooms from long years on the other side of the desk, your skilful practice may appear familiar and deceptively simple. Uninformed about your pupils' prior knowledge and shared history, and about their individual misconceptions and specific learning needs, it is all too easy for a trainee to overlook the ways in which the explanations you frame and the tasks you devise depend not simply on knowledge of the content outlined in an exam specification, but on your developed understandings of how these children learn most effectively, and on your specific awareness of the particular stumbling blocks that they now need to overcome.

While we are certainly not suggesting that effective support for trainees depends on working your way through a checklist of different items, an awareness of the range of different dimensions to which beginners need to attend can help both in pitching your expectations and demands of them appropriately and in structuring the programme that you construct for them in school. It can also help as a diagnostic tool in determining what particular kinds of knowledge or skill they will need to develop in order to respond effectively to a particular classroom dilemma.

The importance of interpretation and judgement

The challenge that teaching presents for beginners arises not just from its dependence on such a wide range of knowledge and skills, but also from the fact that none of them can be effectively developed in isolation from the others. Because teaching and learning are social processes involving a diverse range of individuals, there is a constant interplay between the different knowledge bases on which teachers need to draw. Since teaching needs to be responsive to specific pupils in specific circumstances, it depends fundamentally on a process of selection (determining which features of the situation are most pertinent in deciding what to do), interpretation and judgement. Krievaldt and Turnidge (2013, p 106) refer to this as 'clinical reasoning' and define it as the 'analytical and intuitive cognitive processes that professionals use to arrive at a best judged ethical response in a specific practice-based context'.

The complexity of the classroom

What makes this reasoning so complex – and calls for intuition as much as conscious analysis – is the fact that teachers are rarely dealing with just one individual pupil or seeking to achieve one single objective. Class teaching involves juggling the immediate and longer term needs of up to 30 individual young people, interacting in complex ways with each other as well as with the teacher. Even though we may be able to map out the range of competences and skills that teachers need, and can generate well-grounded propositions and suggestions for practice in relation to each of them, addressing them in isolation does not adequately prepare beginners for the realities of practice in which all of these skills and competences are combined. We cannot offer a codified body of knowledge or a set of routine practices that can be effectively applied in every circumstance. Instead we have to find ways of helping beginners to develop the mental schemas and the dispositions towards learning in complex situations that will enable them to make sense of what is going on and build their capacity to exercise judgement (or 'clinical reasoning') in action.

The challenges that this presents were neatly summed up many years ago by Doyle. For the beginning teachers that he observed on a weekly basis, the most striking features of the classroom were its *'multi-dimensionality, simultaneity and unpredictability'* (Doyle 1977, p 52). Among the range of activities that he noted going on in any lesson, teachers are likely to be

processing subject matter information, judging student abilities, managing classroom groups, coping with emotional responses to events and behaviours, establishing procedures for routine and special assignments, distributing resources and supplies, record-keeping etc.

Moreover, these processes constantly interact with one another: ways of dealing with one dimension (such as distributing resources), for example, have consequences for other dimensions (such as managing classroom groups), and procedures used at one point may establish precedents, shaping pupils' expectations in ways that restrict teachers' options later on. Just one activity, managing a class discussion, requires the teacher to attend simultaneously to

the pace of the interaction, the sequence of students' responses, fairness in selecting students to answer, the quality of individual answers and their relevance to the purposes of the discussion, and the logic and accuracy of content, while at the same time monitoring a wide range of work involvement levels, and anticipating interruptions from internal and external sources.

(Doyle, 1977, p 52)

Reconciling competing concerns

It is not just that teachers are trying to deal with numerous things at once. More than that, Doyle argues that the range of different purposes being served and the variety of events and processes are *'not all necessarily related or even compatible'*. Kennedy, who has examined experienced teachers' ways of thinking about practice, takes up this theme, concluding that teachers are actually trying to address no fewer than six different competing concerns:

- » *covering desirable content;*
- » *fostering student learning;*
- » *increasing students' willingness to participate;*
- » *maintaining lesson momentum;*
- » *creating a civil classroom community; and*
- » *attending to their own cognitive and emotional needs.*

(Kennedy, 2006, p 205)

While, at any particular time, one or more of these concerns might need more attention than others, none of them can ever be wholly neglected. If a pupil asks a fascinating but complex question, for example, the teacher needs to weigh up the trade-off between maintaining lesson momentum and sustaining the pupil's willingness to participate. Particular teaching strategies – such as an investigative or enquiry-based approach to mathematics – might seem desirable because of their potential to stimulate children's curiosity and problem-solving skills, but they are also likely to trigger anxieties (particularly for a beginner) about maintaining momentum and sustaining order, and may even call into question their own cognitive capabilities. That is precisely what happened in the example we cited in the Introduction, when Rhiannon followed the advice of her mentor in setting an exploratory mathematics activity that enthused and animated the pupils, but that quickly proved overwhelming in terms of her ability to respond to the diverse insights and questions that it provoked. She also struggled to manage the levels of frustration and impatience that arose as some pupils pursued less productive avenues and so could not discern the patterns that she had expected them to be able to identify. In closing down the range of options that the pupils could pursue, she chose, at that point, to prioritise lesson momentum and her own cognitive and emotional needs. In the longer term, her desire for security and control meant that while she certainly sought to cover desirable content, she felt that she could not pay as much attention as she wanted to approaches that might have been more effective in stimulating learning or increasing pupils' willingness to participate.

While Rhiannon's experience provides a detailed example of these apparently incompatible objectives, the systematic analysis that we conducted for all the trainees participating in the DEBT research project confirms this impression of learning to teach as an almost impossible juggling task (Burn et al, 2000, 2003). In examining the accounts that the trainees gave of each of their lessons, we identified and categorised all the aims or goals that they were seeking to achieve and all the factors that they took into account in making decisions at the planning stage or during the lesson itself. The sheer range of goals and factors illustrates just how many plates they were trying to keep spinning!

We identified six kinds of goals, listed here in order of the frequency with which they appeared in the trainees' accounts of their lessons.

1. *'Pupil achievement'* encompassed any statement of what the trainees wanted the pupils to achieve. It included *'cognitive'* goals focused on pupils' learning – most obviously the comprehension, retention or use of certain ideas or concepts or items of factual information – along with *'coverage'* of particular content or the generation of some kind of *'product'* – a written explanation, a creative story or poem, a diagram etc.

2. *'Pupil state'* included any goals that were directed towards changing or maintaining a particular affective or emotional state, such as pupils' enthusiasm, interest or confidence.

3. *'Pupil action'* comprised all the trainees' goals related to what the pupils were actually doing – both the general management of their behaviour and their execution of specific instructions.

4. *'Pupil knowledge'* was related to the trainees' concerns to promote pupil learning, but was specifically focused on finding out about the pupils' existing knowledge – determining what they knew already in order to focus on pitching tasks and explanations appropriately.

5. *'Self-learning'* included goals related to the trainees' objectives for their own learning, reflecting their intentions to use the lesson or particular elements of it as an opportunity to focus on a particular aspect of teaching or to practise a particular skill.

6. *'Ingredients'* encompassed any of the trainees' concerns to include a particular strategy or action within the lesson with no justification other than that they regarded it as a necessary or desirable characteristic of a good lesson – a feature or component that simply ought to be included.

Although our categories are slightly different from those used by Kennedy (2006), the same range of potentially competing objectives is clear to see. In seeking to achieve those objectives or to arbitrate between them, the range of factors that the trainees took into account was equally apparent. Overall we identified 12 different kinds of factors, many of which included several distinct sub-categories. The most significant type of factor was (unsurprisingly) the *'pupils'* – which might mean reference to their knowledge or understanding, their actions or behaviour, their affective state or their ability – while the second was the particular *'content'* that they were trying to teach, often with additional reference to *'examination or curricular requirements'*. Beyond these, the trainees considered a wide range of contextual factors – some associated with timing and the sequence of learning (the *'time available'* overall, the specific *'time of day'*, the *'relationship of the particular lesson to the wider scheme of work'*, as well as the *'specific phase'* reached within the lesson) – and others associated with the *'resources'* available and *'material conditions'* (such as classroom layout) or with the *'established routines'* operating in that school. Two other key factors related to them as teachers – one was concerned with general conditions that might apply to any *'teacher'* (such as levels of energy or their own interest in the subject matter) and the other with conditions applying specifically to them as *'trainee teachers'*, which meant, for example, that they were likely to be working in a class that was not their own or that they had very limited knowledge of the pupils.

If a trainee – even in their very first lesson – is trying to achieve six different kinds of goal, it is little wonder that the task appears daunting. If, in seeking to identify the most important priorities among those goals, and in working out how best to achieve those priorities without completely sabotaging the others, that trainee is also trying to take into account up to 12 different factors, it is hardly surprising if they struggle or if early successes in relation to one goal are combined with apparently catastrophic failures in relation to others! The clear challenge for you in supporting trainees' school-based learning is to ensure that they are aware of the complexity of what needs to be learned, but that they are not overwhelmed by it. Designing an effective programme depends on finding ways of managing the complexity so that trainees remain confident that they can succeed, but without distorting or denying its reality in ways that will ultimately inhibit their learning.

The distinctive challenges of learning to teach

Professional knowledge has to be enacted

Not only does the task of teaching rely on a *'spectacular array'* of knowledge and skills – including the ability to juggle an incompatible range of objectives – but the processes by which beginners have to master them will probably be unlike other forms of learning in which they have previously engaged. Professional knowledge, as Buchmann (1984) has declared, is, above all, *'knowledge for action'*, which inevitably means that it has a strong experiential dimension. This is not to claim that direct personal experience is all that is needed, but it is to acknowledge that it is only in the processes of planning, teaching and evaluation that all the other sources of knowledge on which trainees might draw come together in action and acquire meaning. Analysis of the trainees' reflections within the DEBT project makes this point quite emphatically. When we counted up all the references that they made to specific instances of learning, and checked on the sources to which the trainees attributed that learning, we found that 72 per cent of them were ascribed to experience – to their engagement in the processes of planning and teaching.

Of course, teaching is not unique in this respect. Shulman (1998, p 516) points to *'six commonplaces'* shared by all professions, among which he includes:

» *'engagement in practical action'*, hence the need to enact knowledge in practice;

» *'uncertainty'*, caused by the different needs of clients and the non-routine nature of problems, hence the need to develop judgement in applying knowledge;

» *'the importance of experience'* in developing practice, hence the need to learn by reflecting on one's practice and its outcomes.

While it is therefore likely that those trainees who are changing career (as Anita did, from medicine to education) may well already appreciate the experiential dimension of learning to teach, those who have only recently graduated may find it rather more difficult to adjust from a purely academic context in which achievement essentially depends on the mastery and deployment of theoretical knowledge. Many, of course, will welcome the change, relishing the chance to get into the classroom and on with the job, but it is important to acknowledge trainees' lack of familiarity with what this might entail and to take stock of the full range of demands that Shulman's *'commonplaces'* actually imply. Those who have found undergraduate study relatively easy may be taken aback by the challenges of action in the public arena of the classroom and struggle (perhaps for the first time) with what they may have assumed to be simple tasks, such as explanation, instruction or questioning. The very nature of these tasks reminds us again of why developing knowledge for action is so demanding in the context of learning to teach. While all professionals need to be responsive to their particular clients, and therefore rely on the exercise of judgement, most allow for its exercise at a slightly more leisurely pace and in more predictable circumstances, generally with the focus on a single client at a time. Once knowledge for action is recognised to be knowledge for *interaction* (with up to 30 pupils), the characteristic features of classroom processes, as identifed by Doyle – its multi-dimensional, simultaneous and unpredictable nature – make easy or quick success much less likely. Successful graduates, used to high achievement, can find themsleves unprepared for the degree of difficulty that they actually encounter.

Even Hanif – whose successful development we outlined in the Introduction – was taken aback by the number of apparently simple tasks that went wrong in one of his early lessons. Much to Hanif's shame and irritation, his mentor felt he had to intervene even before the lesson began when Hanif tried to bring the class into the room and realised that he was not sure which of the many Year 10 pupils waiting outside actually belonged to the group. Part-way through the lesson Hanif was thrown again by the discovery that he had made a mistake in advising the pupils about which method of data display they should use to answer a particular question. His advice in this instance had effectively contradicted his earlier painstaking explanations. After explicitly acknowledging his error and reiterating the key distinctions that he had sought to establish, he was further embarrassed to realise that he had forgotten to collect a set of angle-measurers from the mathematics office. The delay that this caused meant that setting homework turned, in his words, *'into a bit of a fiasco'*, since the pupils had no time to copy the instructions properly. And in a *'disastrous'* finale, his attempt to chase after three pupils who had chosen to leave before he dismissed the class meant that he failed to organise the collection of the pupils' books and of the angle-measurers. Although he certainly learned from these experiences, Hanif's emphatic insistence as he recounted them that he would never make the same mistake again was an indication of the sense of embarrassment and frustration that they had aroused.

Simple rules of thumb are not enough

The approaches that experienced teachers adopt in order to handle so many competing demands offer important ways forward for beginners, but they can also, unfortunately, complicate the very task of learning from those experienced teachers. Kennedy (2006, p 206) points to two vital characteristics of teachers' practice. One is that they tend to devise collections of ready-made responses to events – habits or *'rules of thumb'* – that reduce the need for extensive thought about each event as it unfolds. These practices become sufficiently automated that they can be sustained without excessive cognitive or emotional burden.

The second is for teachers to *'envision'* their lessons before they enact them. Planning, for experienced teachers, tends not to be a linear process, proceeding logically from learning objectives to specific instructional strategies, but rather *'a process of envisioning, in which teachers "see" what will happen'*. The analogy that Kennedy uses to try to describe this process is that of a play – in which teachers envision successive scenes unfolding, each leading towards the intended denouement. Although the analogy is far from perfect, since teachers certainly cannot script the pupils' responses, the process of mental rehearsal – visualising where the pupils will sit, how the expected patterns of behaviour will be established, how connections will be made and momentum maintained – allows teachers to see how each of their concerns will be addressed. The strength of their vision of the outcome also allows them to adapt the performance as circumstances arise, ensuring that they still arrive at the anticipated denouement.

The implications of these characteristics might seem to be that all the trainees need is a good collection of such *rules of thumb* and plenty of opportunities to observe skilful teachers at work. But while both are indeed vitally important for beginners, they are inadequate as the basis of professional preparation. One reason for this arises directly from the fact that the *rules of thumb* and *visions* on which experienced teachers necessarily come to rely tend to be extremely difficult to articulate and thus to make accessible to others. The other derives from the other three *commonplaces* of professional practice.

In Shulman's (1998, p 516) terms, professions are also distinguished by:

» *'service to society'*, implying an ethical and moral commitment to clients;

» *'a body of scholarly knowledge'* that forms the basis of the entitlement to practice;

» *'the development of a professional community'* that aggregates and shares knowledge and develops professional standards.

The *'moral commitment'* that teachers have to ensuring the best outcomes for all their pupils means that it is not enough, even for beginners, simply to be able to follow instructions or to replicate what they have seen others do. They need to be able to evaluate the outcomes of their actions, in relation to the range of objectives with which teachers are concerned, and on a range of competing timescales. Given the inevitable tensions between different objectives, beginners also need to be able to recognise how particular practices have prioritised one outcome over another, and to be able to justify those choices with a clear understanding of their implications. They are unlikely to be able to do so if they are unaware of the nature and strength of the evidence on which those practices have been based. That is why Shulman also emphasises the importance of the *'body of scholarly knowledge'* on which the *'entitlement to practice'* is based. The fact that a particular practice appears to work in their mentor's classroom offers a trainee an invaluable starting point, but it is not sufficient either as a warrant for the trainee to adopt it or to ensure that they will know how to adapt it appropriately, if it does not seem to work for them.

Questioning is an obvious example where practices widely used by teachers that meet certain key objectives in terms of sustaining momentum and maintaining order – such as inviting students to raise their hands to volunteer answers to quick-fire questions and only accepting responses from those complying with that instruction – have been found to generate very limited insights into what pupils across a class have actually learnt or now understand. They thus tend to serve only the more confident and higher attaining pupils (Black and Wiliam, 1998; Black et al, 2002). Strategies that were subsequently developed to ensure that more pupils' ideas could be revealed – such as giving pupils thinking time or the opportunity to discuss their responses with a partner, selecting individuals at random, or seeking written answers from everyone on individual whiteboards – can certainly be demonstrated or taught as routine practices or *'rules of thumb'*. But if trainees are not also given access to the evidence basis on which hands-up questioning has been challenged, they may quickly be tempted to revert to it if they happen to select a pupil who is very slow to respond or they find that the pupils start messing about with the whiteboards.

The way in which Black et al (2003) worked with teachers in light of their original findings about the importance of formative assessment to develop a wide range of strategies that gave teachers new ways of regularly tapping into all pupils' existing and developing understandings also serves to illustrate Shulman's sixth dimension of professional practice. Teaching is undertaken as part of a *'community'* in which new knowledge is built and shared, and in which standards are collectively developed. Individual experts can offer a wealth of expertise to beginners, but no individual's lone claim is an adequate basis for professional practice. Nor can a single *'rule of thumb'* offer adequate guidance for practice in all contexts. That is why Hammerness and her colleagues map out teachers' expertise in terms of two dimensions – those of *'efficiency'* and *'innovation'*. While Kennedy's (2006) *'rules of thumb'* serve the interests of efficiency, giving teachers the ability to perform particular tasks without having to devote too many attentional resources to achieve them, they also require the capacity to innovate: to *'move beyond existing routines… to rethink key ideas, practices, and even values in order to respond to novel situations'* (Hammerness et al, 2005, pp 358–9).

This need for innovation and the ways in which professional standards change in response both to new research and changing classroom contexts mean that trainees are effectively having to learn on two different timescales. Hagger and McIntyre (2006, p 37) capture them both in their list of the tasks to be achieved in terms of trainees' classroom expertise. Not only do they need to develop an *'initial level of teaching competence'* sufficient for them to practise in their training or placement school(s); they also need to develop a *'capacity for continued professional development'*, enabling them to go on learning as a teacher in new contexts, and the *'capacity for critical engagement with suggested innovations in classroom pratice'*. But before turning to the challenges of asking critical questions about practices that they are advised to adopt, it is important to pick up on the second problem associated with the way in which experienced teachers' professional knowledge is stored and deployed as *'rules of thumb'* and lesson *'visions'*: the difficulty of making such knowledge explicit.

Expertise revealed in practice is difficult to articulate

Despite all there is to be learnt from it, the fluency of experienced teachers' practice means that beginners often report feeling bored by classroom observation. As we have already noted, what they see seems obvious to them; what they cannot see is all the knowledge embedded in the thinking that underpins the teacher's practice. They may assume that they understand what is going on, yet *'even the most experienced observer can actually make only very inadequate guesses when observing teachers at work'* and seeking to determine what they are trying to do and why (Hagger and McIntyre, 2006, p 47).

The answer, surely, might seem to be for the experienced teachers to tell them – to share their objectives and intended strategies beforehand and to offer some kind of commentary on particular aspects or critical incidents afterwards. Yet, precisely because experienced teachers have drawn on their store of knowledge and experience to develop shorthand *'rules of thumb'* – regular patterns and routines for accomplishing certain kinds of tasks, about which they no longer need to deliberate – they too can tend to take their expertise for granted. They have so efficiently drawn on different insights and balanced competing priorities that their routine practices can seem as obvious and uncomplicated to them as they do to the beginner, leaving them struggling to identify what exactly it is that they could usefully share. This phenomenon is not confined to teaching. Hargreaves and his colleagues, who were studying medical education, noticed that, despite widespread consensus about the value to junior doctors of the chance to learn from observation of experienced consultants at work on the wards, the junior doctors were routinely left guessing about the grounds on which the consultants had made their clinical judgements. Because the consultants took their judgements for granted, they rarely offered any explanation for them. Hargreaves et al (1997) eventually concluded that the junior doctors would have to be encouraged to ask – a decision that we too have taken in seeking to equip trainees to learn as effectively as they can from experienced teachers' craft knowledge (Hagger et al, 1993; Hagger, 1997; Hagger and McIntyre, 2006).

If that were not challenging enough, other studies of work-based learning have also shown that when experienced practioners *do* talk about their practice within the workplace, they often discuss it in terms of *espoused theories* (the principles that they believe they are following or assume will give credibility to their practice) rather than the nuanced and much more highly contextualised *theories-in-use* on which they actually rely. As Eraut (2000) has noted, language used in the workplace may *'serve purposes other than making knowledge of actions explicit'*. Such discourse may be used both:

(1) to provide a defensible account rather than a description of practitioners' actions and (2) to create an impression of professional control over situations which inspire confidence in them as persons. It may seek to disguise rather than to share uncertainty and risk-taking.

Eraut (2000, p 120)

This is perhaps particularly likely to happen where mentors, especially those new to the role, assume that assured declarations of principle or reference to particular theoretical ideas will boost their trainees' confidence in their knowledge and understanding. While trainees certainly need to know how research-based understandings can inform practice, they will not really be able to make sense of what they see unless the explanations that they are offered actually reflect the highly nuanced and context-specific understandings on which that practice has been based.

Asking critical questions demands both sensitivity and self-awareness

Getting trainees to ask specific questions about the details of what they see experienced teachers do has been shown to be very effective in giving them access to these much more nuanced understandings. But even a genuinely open question, seeking understanding, can be difficult to phrase in a way that does not sound negative or presumptuous, especially when uttered by a newcomer. Even when prompted simply by curiosity, the question *'Why did you do that?'* can all too easily be interpreted as implying some kind of judgement. We have found that trainees need to work extraordinarily hard to reassure the experts from whom they are seeking to learn, cushioning their questions by expressions of their interest and admiration in order to get the best out of them (Hagger, 1997). *'I was really impressed by the way you got that student back on track – how did you…?'* or *'I was intrigued by the fact that you jumped straight from that activity to the plenary. Why did you decide…?'* work much more effectively than a blunt *'Why?'*. Their power also lies in their highly specific focus. Looking at detailed instances makes it much more likely that experienced teachers will be able to identify and to articulate the richness and range of the knowledge on which they actually drew, albeit essentially intuitively, in making their decisions.

Ultimately, of course, trainees do need to go beyond simply seeking understanding of others' rationales. As we have argued earlier, they need to be able to subject the practices that they adopt to critical scrutiny, ensuring that they are rationally and ethically defensible in light of the best evidence that we have about how children learn, and with due regard to the specific features of the particular context. Mentors and other experienced colleagues working with beginners are right in thinking that the practices that they offer to beginners will indeed be closely scrutinised. The real task is not actually to prevent this but to ensure that it is done as sensitively and rigorously as possible; that is, with due regard to the full range of criteria that professional practice demands and an acknowledgement that competing goals cannot all be satisfied at once, but need to be addressed systematically over time. As Hagger and McIntyre (2006, p 58) have noted, while some of these criteria are *'properly of a practical nature – their feasiblity given the time, space and resources available, and indeed the trainees' current level of expertise'* – others may be concerned with *'the values and assumptions embedded within the practices, the purposes for which they are most appropriate and the circumstances in which they tend to be effective'*. Beginners need to be encouraged to look across all the relevant criteria rather than relying on just one or two. They also need considerable encouragement to apply the same judgements to the ideas that they themselves bring with them to their training. It demands enormous self-awareness for anyone to recognise the strength of their preconceptions and to subject them to critical scrutiny – a process in which trainees are only likely to engage if they can see that those advising them are willing to ask the same questions of their own preferred practices.

Sustaining a dual identity as teacher and learner

In elaborating the challenges of learning to teach, we have summed up the range of demands that teaching itself presents and have explored particular problems associated with learning from experience in the complex, dynamic and unpredictable context of the classroom. But to appreciate fully the demands that trainees face in learning to teach, it is also important to acknowledge the tensions inherent in the *dual* role that they are expected to play as both teachers *and* learners.

The very idea of being a teacher carries with it an assumption about the capacity to lead others. A teacher is not only expected to possess superior knowledge of the subject to be learned but also the ability to direct and manage the learning of others. It is not surprising that trainees, anxious to be seen and respected, not least by their pupils, as figures of authority within the classroom, feel under enormous pressure to demonstrate their competence. Anita's sense of anguish about her classroom *'mistakes'* was particularly pronounced because she had become accustomed in her previous career to being seen as an accomplished professional; but even Hanif squirmed with embarrassment as he recounted the list of oversights and errors that he was *'determined to ensure never happened again'*. Teachers are supposed to know what they are doing and to arrive fully prepared with the resources they need; they should not have to rely on others coming to their rescue or find themselves apologising to pupils for errors in their explanations. Hanif's concern to get it right was not simply motivated by concern for the pupils' learning (though that was undoubtedly tremendously important to him); it was also about protecting his own developing identity as a teacher.

Research in teacher education *'increasingly emphasises the importance of teacher identity'* (Pillen et al, 2013, p 240), and central to the development of any beginner's sense of identity is the way in which they are seen by others. Wanting to demonstrate their credibility can therefore make some trainees very reluctant to engage in activities which mark them out as novices. Yet these are the very actions that are likely to be most useful to them, such as observing experienced teachers and asking specific questions about the thinking behind their decisions or seeking advice in relation to their own planning and detailed feedback on their own teaching (if it is not naturally forthcoming). Anita's heightened anxiety about her identity as a teacher made her particularly anxious about being observed or accepting advice; what she craved was evidence that her teaching colleagues regarded her as competent. Her favourite teacher in the department, she explained, *'never told me what I was to do; she never gave me any support, and that was fine because what she gave me was trust'*. Rob, with previous overseas teaching experience, was much more self-assured. Even so, he took no action to seek further feedback or to draw attention to his continuing need for guidance when he felt that it was inappropriate for his mentor to have reduced the number of lessons he was observing.

The sense of relief that trainees experience when they feel that they have been judged to be essentially competent unfortunately makes it much more likely that they will achieve only the first of the three tasks that Hagger and McIntyre (2006, p 37) outline in relation to the development of trainees' classroom expertise. While they may develop *'an initial level of teaching competence sufficient for them to practise in their training or placement school(s)'*, without adequate support in sustaining their identity as learners and not just as teachers, they may well fail to develop the capacities needed *'for continued professional development enabling them to go on learning as a teacher in new contexts, and for critical engagement with suggested innovations in classroom practice'*. This risk of stalling has been highlighted by Furlong and Maynard (1995, p 89), who refer to trainees *'hitting a plateau'* when they have learned to replicate experienced teachers' behaviour without developing a *'full appreciation of the professional knowledge that underlies it'* or of how it may need to be adapted in different circumstances. It is the same risk that prompted Zeichner to warn against the dangers of judging the effectiveness of a school placement simply on the basis of the trainee's classroom performance, insisting that:

Unless the practicum helps to teach prospective teachers how to take control of their own professional development and to learn how to continue learning, it is miseducative, no matter how successful the teacher might be in the short run.

(Zeichner, 1996, p 217)

The temptation to focus on achieving and demonstrating competence as quickly as possible, even at the expense of more secure understandings and the capacity to go on learning, is perhaps even more pronounced now than it was when Zeichner first issued that warning. The sociologist Stephen Ball (2003) is among those who have charted the rise of a culture of *'performativity'* associated with recent reform movements in education (and across the public sector) that are predicated on constant monitoring and judgement, using comparison and competition to drive up standards. The assumptions that underpin this approach to reform mean that it is not only trainees who feel that they need to demonstrate their competence; experienced teachers may well feel a similar sense of insecurity – *'a sense of being constantly judged in different ways'* (Ball, 2003, p 220) – that encourages them too to focus on demonstrating what they believe is currently required of them, rather than on evaluating the impact of their actions in relation to the purposes that they are seeking to achieve. Given this emphasis on performance, it is hardly surprising if that is what trainees come to assume matters most.

The challenge therefore in supporting trainees to move beyond initial competence, developing their capacity to go on learning and to ask critical questions of suggested innovations, is that of persuading them to go on acting in ways that will mark them out as learners. Asking specific questions of experienced teachers' practice, planning collaboratively with them, continuing to be observed and discussing those observations with experienced colleagues are the best ways both of gaining access to the professional knowledge of experienced teachers and of learning to ask critical questions about their own practice. But sustaining such practices is only going to be possible if you can help trainees to reconcile the tension between being seen as a teacher and continuing to act as a learner.

Fortunately, resolution is possible; however, much depends on you, the experienced teacher. If your own identity as a teacher clearly also embodies that of a learner, trainees will have the chance to see that they do not need to shed the latter in order to embrace the former. By demonstrating that your expertise depends on a continuing commitment to learning – not just modelling processes of adaptation and evaluation but sharing your own questions, dilemmas and doubts – it is much more likely that your trainees' sense of professional identity will come to include both the dimensions of *'adaptive expertise'*, not just *'efficiency'* but also *'innovation'* – the capacity to generate new solutions (Hammerness et al, 2005).

IN A **NUTSHELL**

The nature of teachers' professional knowledge and the ways in which it has to be acquired thus present a range of challenges for school-based teacher educators. The first is to ensure that trainees are aware of the complexity of what needs to be learnt but are not overwhelmed by it, giving them confidence that they can succeed without distorting or denying its reality in ways that ultimately inhibit their learning. The second is to find ways of making your own expertise accessible to them, not simply as practices to be replicated nor as espoused theories, but as a process of well-informed analytical reasoning, albeit one now practised with a fluency that makes it seem like little more than intuition. The third is to find ways of validating trainees' emerging identity as teachers that do not impede their continued learning. While respect for them and sensitivity are vital in that task, the most powerful resource you have is the model that you present to them, demonstrating in your own commitment to learning the extent to which adaptive expertise depends on the ability to keep asking critical questions.

REFLECTIONS ON **CRITICAL ISSUES**

- *Teachers need three kinds of knowledge bases – knowledge of learners and learning; knowledge of subject matter and curriculum goals; and knowledge of teaching – but each encompasses a wide range of different dimensions and none of them can be neatly applied.*
- *The diverse needs of specific learners in particular contexts and the range of competing goals that teachers are seeking to achieve simultaneously means that teachers' expertise essentially depends on a process of selection, interpretation and judgement.*
- *Professional learning is not only about learning for action; much of it has to be learned in action. One of the most valuable resources for beginners, ie professional teachers' knowledge-in-use, is very difficult for beginners to access.*
- *The desire to secure their identity as a teacher and to be accepted as such by pupils and colleagues may lead trainees into simple imitation rather than the development of genuinely adaptive expertise.*

CRITICAL **ISSUES**

- *What impact do beginning teachers' preconceptions have on their views of what they are going to learn and how best they can do that?*
- *Are there any common patterns in beginning teachers' development that could be used to inform the kinds of structured support offered to them at different stages?*
- *How much variation is there in the ways in which beginning teachers draw on and make sense of their classroom experience?*
- *How important are the affective or emotional dimensions of learning to teach and in what ways do they influence beginning teachers' development?*

The impact of beginning teachers' preconceptions

Preconceptions shaping beginners' views of what they need to learn

Teaching is perhaps unique among the professions in that all those seeking to join it have already served a long *'apprenticeship of observation'* (Lortie, 1975). Virtually all novice teachers come into school with more than ten years' experience in classrooms: experience not simply as observers, judging the quality of their teachers' performance, but direct experience of its impact on their own learning. Unsurprisingly, this gives many beginning teachers tremendous confidence in their ability to judge the nature of effective teaching. Even if they recognise that their experience may not hold true for all learners, their conceptions are still firmly rooted and difficult to dislodge. As Anita declared at the start of her training year, '*I have a very fixed idea of the kind of teacher I would like to be, and what makes a good teacher*'.

While most trainees point to the inspiration of a favourite teacher whom they may be seeking to emulate – the *'remarkable English teacher whose love for her subject captivated me'* or the science teacher who *'always came up with answers to my questions and never dismissed my ideas'* – the long apprenticeship that they have served can, on occasion, also give rise to deeply entrenched negative images – models of teaching that some trainees passionately reject.

Their own education is not the only prior experience on which beginners' assumptions about effective teaching may be based. Most aspiring teachers cite previous teaching roles that they have adopted – perhaps informally within their own families, as young leaders within voluntary groups, such as the guides or scouts, or more formal responsibility for training others within their previous employment. Many have gone further, testing the strength of their resolve by first working as a teaching assistant or cover supervisor. Others – like Rob, who spent two years teaching in West Africa – have undertaken voluntary work in teaching roles or completed short courses in teaching English as a foreign language, equipping them to work in language schools within the United Kingdom or overseas. While they may not run as deep as the beliefs shaped over long years as a pupil, ideas and principles derived from these subsequent teaching experiences undoubtedly also influence the assumptions of beginning teachers, shaping the lens through which they view, not only the nature of teaching and the value of specific pedagogical strategies, but also the pupils that they encounter.

Most common among the trainees within the DEBT project was a tendency to conceive of *'good teaching'* in terms of teachers' personal characteristics (such as enthusiasm or compassion) and to talk about the practices of established teachers in terms of an undifferentiated *'teaching style'* – demonstrating little awareness of the need for a flexible repertoire of strategies and careful judgement about when and how to apply them (Younger et al, 2004). Less common, but certainly very pronounced when they did arise, were assumptions about particular teaching strategies. One trainee's rejection of group work was rooted in her frustration as a pupil at being required to work with unco-operative peers in a badly managed environment. Although she had taken part in highly productive group seminars at university, the constant disruption of her secondary school history lessons meant that she simply rejected the idea that discussion could be of any value for younger pupils.

While her anxiety made her cautious, other trainees drawing on their own experience may be over-optimistic, as this quotation from a mathematics trainee illustrates:

Teaching is really cool because ... you get to talk about something you're really interested in all the time. And you have this captive audience who not only has to sit there, but basically wants to find out what you're saying. Some kids don't, but by and large the kids are in school and know that they're there to learn, and are happy that that is the ways things are.

It may be tempting to be dismissive of such views, confident that the trainee will quickly be disabused of the assumption that most pupils are eagerly awaiting all that he has to share. However, for the mentor supporting his learning, it is much more important to recognise his current conception of teaching as *telling* and to identify a possible tendency to divide pupils into distinct categories – those who want to learn and those who do not – rather than recognising the range of different influences on students' motivation and capacity to learn, and the strategies that teachers might employ to enhance them both.

The need to take account of learners' preconceptions is, of course, far from being a new idea. It is one of the three essential principles identified in Donovan and Bransford's distillation of research into pupils' learning:

[Pupils] come to the classroom with preconceptions about how the world works. If their initial understanding is not engaged, they may fail to grasp the new concepts and information, or

they may learn them for purposes of a test but revert to their preconceptions outside the classroom.

(Donovan and Bransford, 2005, p 1)

Just as it is with pupils, so it is with teachers. If we do not acknowledge the power of the ideas that trainees bring with them and fail to find appropriate points of connection – engaging their *'initial understanding'* – any advice that we give is likely to fall on deaf ears. Trainees may comply with our demands and enact the suggestions that we offer, but if those suggestions do not resonate with their own assumptions, they are much less likely to make sense of or persevere with them. As Lacey (1977) first explained, they may simply adopt them as a form of *'strategic compliance'*, abandoning them again when we are no longer watching. Once we have some insight into our trainees' existing ideas about good teaching and their expectations of pupils, we are much better equipped to help them first to identify, and then to evaluate, the grounds on which those ideas are based. We can also pinpoint the kinds of evidence that they are most likely to find persuasive and encourage them to reflect on the values implicit within them. Only by eliciting and paying serious attention to their existing views can we help the trainees to begin to interrogate them.

Preconceptions about the best ways of learning to teach

Other kinds of preconception also exert a powerful influence on the way in which beginners respond to their training programme and to the opportunities, challenges and support that you provide. In some cases these ideas too are rooted in particular prior experiences, such as Rob's teaching in West Africa. In others they reflect a more widespread assumption among beginners that because they are essentially familiar with classroom practices they will quickly make sense of what is going on. Unless ideas and assumptions of this kind are also explicitly acknowledged and examined, their influence may constrain your trainees' learning.

Rob, as we explained in the Introduction, readily accepted the idea that one could always go on improving as a teacher, but rarely made any deliberate plans to develop particular skills or experiment with new strategies. He tended instead to rely on a retrospective process of reflection, identifying and remedying the weaknesses in specific lesson plans once he had taught them. This approach, we realised, was entirely consistent with – and essentially shaped by – the strategies that he had adopted when teaching abroad:

I would teach the same lesson three times in a week – to three different classes in each year group. And I know that every time I taught the lesson it got better, simply because I would think, 'That didn't really work. How can I change it?' And they would only be small changes, but it would improve the lesson immensely.

Obviously, this kind of repeated refinement has much to recommend it – and it served Rob well in the early stages of his training year. However, the lack of forward planning and the self-reliance that it inspired proved much more limiting as time went on. Although Rob intimated to the research team that he would have welcomed more extensive feedback, he made no formal request to his mentor for more observation. Nor did he ever expand his reflections beyond what was immediately apparent, as he might have done, for example, by asking pupils for feedback. As time went on, his outlook became increasingly limited.

As Rob's assumptions about learning to teach illustrate, the notion of learning by doing is a particularly powerful preconception about the process of learning to teach – one that is perfectly well justified, as we noted in Chapter 2, because of the way in which professional knowledge has to be enacted. However, learning from experience, as Rob's example suggests, can have quite particular meanings and may, in fact, be understood by different people in very different ways, not all of which are equally helpful (as we explore more fully below). Other common preconceptions that can act as barriers to beginners' learning include the assumptions that determining what works and what does not is an essentially simple process, or that learning from observation will be similarly straightforward. Trainees holding such views are much less likely to recognise the importance of asking questions about the teachers' objectives and how they were determined, or about how their original planning decisions were related to those objectives, and whether or how they were adapted as the lesson unfolded. Without that perspective, trainees may remain entirely unaware of the competing objectives with which teachers routinely have to deal (as explored in Chapter 2). They may also fall into the trap of seeking to imitate actions without understanding their purpose. Frustrated in that endeavour, they may equally well conclude that further observation has little to offer them – and so rule out the gains that might later be made from it, as their awareness of specific challenges and their understanding of teachers' decision-making processes deepen.

Typical trajectories?

Just as you need to be aware of those individual differences between beginning teachers who are shaped by their prior experiences and particular preconceptions, so you need to be wary of assuming that they will all follow a similar trajectory once embarked on their training. While extensive research in different contexts does identify a number of typical features in trainees' development over time, it also reveals the complexity of trainees' thinking – the range of issues with which they may be grappling at any one point – and the extent of variation between individuals. While it certainly helps to be aware of the kind of trajectory that your trainees may well follow, you need to be alert both to their particular starting points and to the considerable scope that there is for deviation. It is important not to let your own preconceptions about trainees' learning blind you to their specific concerns and developmental priorities.

Common stages in beginning teachers' development

In mapping out a typical trajectory of beginning teachers' developing concerns, the model developed by Fuller and Bown (1975) more than 40 years ago has proved remarkably robust. While this undoubtedly reflects the painstaking process of research and refinement originally invested in developing the model, it also illustrates the model's resonance with the expectations of successive generations of teacher educators. The model suggests that the concerns of beginning teachers move 'outwards': concerns about self and their survival are succeeded by concerns about classroom tasks, which in turn give way to concerns about pupils and their learning.

Twenty years later, Furlong and Maynard (1995) developed a more elaborate model, based on several inter-related studies of primary trainees in South Wales. Although they include more stages of development, and sound a cautious note about assuming that progress will necessarily be steady, the same broad trend can be discerned in their five stages.

1. *'Early idealism'* – in which trainees tend to identify quite closely with the pupils and seek inspiration in the example of significant teachers recalled from their own schooldays. Their analysis of these teachers (as we noted, in considering trainees' preconceptions) tends to be framed in terms of the teachers' personality and the relationships that they established, rather than reference to the planning and structure of their lessons or their pedagogical strategies.

2. *'Personal survival'* – in which trainees tend to feel vulnerable and crave the assurance of being seen as a teacher. They are therefore keen to fit in and become anxious about securing effective control of their classes.

3. *'Dealing with difficulties'* – in which the emphasis is on establishing themselves as a teacher by implementing specific policies (particularly in relation to managing pupils' behaviour) and demonstrating their ability to organise and execute different kinds of learning activities.

4. *'Hitting a plateau'* – in which progress may stall as the trainees demonstrate their competence and confidence in running a classroom, and implementing different kinds of activity. Only if they are sufficiently challenged and encouraged to look more closely at the pupils' experience and the evidence of their learning will they move on.

5. *'Moving on'* – the final phase in which they are able and willing to adapt their teaching in response to critical evaluation of the pupils' needs and their ongoing learning.

The stories of trainees presented earlier in this book resonate in many respects with the different phases outlined in this model. Many of the preconceptions that we discussed reflect *'early idealism'*. Anita's sense of shock and fragility after losing the public acknowledgement accorded to her previous professional competence clearly reveals her preoccupation with *'personal survival'*, as she struggled to establish a new teacher identity. Hanif's frustration with his early organisational difficulties is prompted by his rapid realisation of just how much he needs to learn in order to ensure a smooth-running lesson. The way in which Rob's professional learning stalled once his mentor had judged him to be essentially competent provides a compelling demonstration of the risks of plateauing.

It is therefore worth planning your response as a mentor to the needs of a trainee expressing the kinds of concern that characterise each of these phases. But the findings of the DEBT project clearly demonstrate that while these phases may all feature at some point in an individual's trajectory, few trainees actually work through them in this neatly ordered sequence. Many of those who have drawn on stage models of development reach the same conclusion that the idea of sequential stages does not adequately capture the complexity of individuals' development over time (Conway and Clark, 2003; Watzke, 2007). They particularly warn teacher educators against adopting a deficit model of their trainees that fails to acknowledge just how much they may be dealing with at any one time

(Guillaume and Rudney, 1993; Pendry, 1997) – a warning that echoes our own advice (Burn et al, 2003; Mutton et al, 2011).

The limitations of conventional stage theories of development

Far from an exclusive concern with self, the overwhelming impression that we gained of the trainees' thinking as they set out to plan their very first lessons (as we explained in Chapter 2) was the *breadth* of their thinking. While their ambitions might be seen as unhelpfully idealistic – as in Rhiannon's use of exploratory investigation in her very first lesson – they also reveal the strength of their commitment to the pupils' learning. Despite the organisational *disasters* of Hanif's first lesson, he certainly did not stop thinking about the different levels of understanding that were revealed in the pupils' facial expressions, and in their questions and responses to particular tasks. Just as he registered that he should have collected a set of angle-measurers before the lesson, so he recognised that he needed to address the confusion that some of the pupils revealed about the kinds of data that could legitimately be presented using a histogram.

An early focus on pupil learning

In their early focus on pupil learning, Rhiannon and Hanif were far from unique – as our analysis of the trainees' aims and subsequent lesson evaluations reveal. As explained in Chapter 2, we identified six different types of aims in the trainees' accounts of their planning and teaching: four concerned with the pupils (focusing on their achievement, their affective state, their behaviour and their prior knowledge), one concerned with their own learning and one related to their vision of what should be included in a good lesson. While the proportion of the trainees' aims that were concerned with pupil progress clearly increased over the course of the second term (accounting for two-thirds of their references to lesson aims in the two rounds of interviews conducted during that period), it was also true that more than half of the trainees' aims even in the *first* round of interviews were similarly concerned with pupil progress or achievement. We also analysed the terms in which the trainees evaluated their lessons on each occasion. Again, while there was an obvious shift as the year went on, with the trainees increasingly looking beyond their own actions to consider what the pupils were taking from the experience, almost half of their judgements in the first round of interviews were similarly concerned with the pupils, suggesting that the trainees were far from being exclusively concerned with their own performance. Even if your trainees do not yet know how to achieve their aims, it is important to acknowledge and build on their early concerns for pupil progress.

Simultaneous rather than sequential concerns

A second cautionary note is about not assuming that beginning teachers deal with the different issues that confront them in a sequential manner, addressing issues of behaviour management first, for example, and then moving on to focus on task design, before finally focusing effectively on pupil learning. Although we did see an increase in the proportion of trainees' aims concerned with pupils' achievement, this was accompanied by a *parallel* increase in the proportion of aims focused on the pupils' actions (their behaviour and the extent to which they were on task). Our third round of interviews, which marked a peak in terms of the proportion of aims and evaluative statements focused on pupils' achievement, also included the highest proportion of references to pupils' actions or behaviour as factors taken into account by the trainees. Pendry (1997, p 206) reached a similar conclusion from a small-scale study of history teachers' lesson planning – noting that once they were in school full time, trainees were attending simultaneously to *'all three of these things: management, teaching and learning'*. Watzke, who tracked 79 beginning teachers for two years, argued that rather than being dealt with in a chronological sequence, beginning teachers' concerns essentially recur. Instead of focusing first on managerial aspects of teaching, those supporting beginners' learning therefore need to *'scaffold linkages between pupil learning, learning theory and instructional practices'* (Watzke, 2007, p 106).

The different dimensions of learning from experience

Perhaps the most important example of individual variation in relation to a common theme relates to the ways in which beginner teachers understand and engage in the process of learning from experience. The assumption that this is essentially how they will learn is not only deeply rooted, but also extremely well founded, as we confirmed in Chapter 2. Seventy-two per cent of the specific instances of learning to which the trainees in the DEBT project referred were attributed to experience. As Eraut has pointed out, that finding is entirely to be expected:

[A]lthough many areas of professional knowledge are dependent on some understanding of relevant public codified knowledge found in books and journals, professional knowledge is constructed through experience and its nature depends on the cumulative acquisition, selection and interpretation of that experience.

(Eraut, 1994, p 19–20)

Experience is vital, since it is in the processes of planning, teaching and evaluation that all the other sources of knowledge on which beginning teachers might draw come together in action and acquire meaning.

However, while all the trainees whom we were tracking claimed to *'learn from experience'*, more detailed analysis of their accounts made it clear that learning from experience meant different sorts of things on different occasions or – more obviously – to different trainees. The simple category *experience* actually encompassed a wide variety of learning processes that included, for example:

» the implementation of specific teaching tasks outlined in their department's scheme of work, and careful evaluation of the outcomes, drawing on a range of evidence;

» trainees' instinctive judgements about a plan's effectiveness based on how *'comfortable'* they felt with it;

» deliberate experimentation with, and subsequent evaluation of, ideas suggested to the trainees by their university-based tutors;

» reflections – often quite emotionally driven – on what they realised they still had to learn about engaging pupils' interest or classroom management.

From our analysis of these wide-ranging processes and of the ways in which the trainees embarked on and responded to them, we eventually identified five key themes or dimensions according to which their approaches to learning from experience could be categorised. The most effective way of capturing these five dimensions was as *'opposable orientations'* (Bullough et al, 2004, p 368) – each representing different aspects of the trainees' approach. These five dimensions are summarised in Table 3.1.

Table 3.1 Learning from experience: five dimensions according to which trainees' orientations may differ.

Dimension	Orientation			
Aspiration The extent of the trainee's aspirations for their own and their pupils' learning	Satisfaction with current level of achievement	←	→	Aspirational both as learners and teachers
Intentionality The extent to which the trainees' learning is planned	Reactive	←	→	Deliberative
Frame of reference The value that the trainee ascribes to looking beyond their experience in order to make sense of it	Exclusive reliance on the experience of classroom teaching	←	→	Drawing on a range of sources to shape and make sense of experience
Response to feedback The trainee's disposition towards receiving feedback and the value that they attribute to it	Tendency to be disabled by critical feedback	←	→	Effective use of feedback to further learning
Attitude to context Attitude to the positions in which trainees find themselves and the approaches that they take to the school context	Tendency to regard the context as constraining	←	→	Acceptance of the context and ability to capitalise on it

Source: Table adapted from Hagger et al (2008).

Current dispositions rather than fixed characteristics

In using the term *'orientations'*, we are not suggesting that these are fixed characteristics of each trainee, rather that they reflect their current disposition at a particular point in time. Indeed, as we used the dimensions to help us to identify and map the attitudes revealed in each interview over the course of the training year (and for the two years after that), we could discern both specific differences on particular occasions and, in certain cases, clear trends over time. These trends are particularly evident in Rhiannon's case when her initial aspirations were significantly reduced in response to the early challenges that she encountered. They rose again, however, during the course of her second year in teaching, in response to the structured programme of shared observations that her head of department had put in place. This programme also prompted her to adopt a more experimental approach to her teaching, thereby promoting a much more deliberative orientation than she had ever shown before.

In tracking all 24 trainees, we became increasingly aware of the ways in which their current dispositions towards learning from experience interacted with the support structures that they encountered in their schools. In some cases the effects were mutually reinforcing: Hanif's high aspirations and deliberative approach to his own learning were sustained by regular support, as well as by fresh stimuli and new sources of challenge. Rob's tendency to restrict his frame of reference to his own classroom, adapting and tweaking what he was doing on a trial and error basis, was compounded by a mentor who essentially withdrew once he had judged Rob to be a competent teacher. In other cases, like Rhiannon's, we could see how particular experiences and carefully targeted interventions could help to change a beginner's orientation. In a few cases, we also saw how trainees' positive orientations impacted on the departments in which they were placed, transforming not just their own, but other teachers' opportunities to learn more effectively. It is precisely because of this potential for change that you need both to identify your trainees' current dispositions towards learning from experience and, where necessary, seek to promote more positive orientations.

Aspiration

Obviously, the extent of trainees' ambitions acts as a powerful determinant of their learning. Those with high aspirations – expressed either in relation to their pupils or in terms of their own development – may be willing to invest a great deal of effort in the process of learning to teach. The relationship between aspiration and action is not, however, straightforward. Early idealism can often be quite unfocused, as in Anita's case, who was concerned essentially with the quality of her relationships with the pupils and the development of their creativity. Striving for perfection in ways that fail to acknowledge the competing demands that teachers face and the need for conscious compromise in relation to one goal in order to achieve another is a maladaptive practice (Rice and Lapsley, 2001) that can quickly lead to frustration and, sometimes, despair. High levels of aspiration, *in themselves*, are no guarantee of success (though genuine concern for pupils' progress is an essential prerequisite); it is necessary to consider the *relationship* between each of the five different dimensions.

At one end of the spectrum we found low levels of aspiration, which obviously impact on trainees' expectations of themselves and of their pupils. Sometimes they reflect a lack, or loss, of confidence, as happened in Rhiannon's case when her initial hopes of encouraging independent investigation were frustrated by her inability (at that point) to deal with the range of different ideas generated by her pupils. But relatively low aspirations may *also* arise from feelings of confidence, as evident in Rob's tendency to gauge the success of a lesson in terms of how *'comfortable'* he felt with it. In both cases, the trainees' development exhibited the kind of *'plateauing'* identified by Furlong and Maynard (1995). Although Rhiannon obviously learned how to manage her classes effectively, she then made few efforts to broaden her repertoire of teaching strategies (a process on which she only embarked towards the end of her NQT year). Rob was only inspired to focus seriously on his own development when he was faced with a new curriculum or took on responsibilities beyond the classroom.

Of course, aspirations may also weaken simply because trainees are nearing the end of a placement. One science trainee within the DEBT project, previously enthusiastic about experimenting with different teaching approaches with a lower-attaining class of 14–15-year-olds, acknowledged in the final interview that he was no longer trying to develop his own teaching:

I'm just looking to the end now, and thinking it's nearly all over, and I'm not as focused as I was... Last term there was a lot more experience of learning going on, whereas now I'm just going through it, going through the motions a bit more I suppose.

While this sense of things coming to an end may well not apply to those following employment-based routes, they too will be subject to the usual rhythms of the school year.

At the opposite end of the continuum, an aspirational orientation is one in which boundaries are constantly being pushed, and trainees are explicitly aware of the risks of complacency. Their aspiration may be focused on the strategies that the trainees are developing or on the pupils' learning. Even when there is a tension between the aspiration to achieve things in certain ways and the level of competence needed to make this feasible, the critical factor is that the desire to improve and develop is expressed in aspirational terms, as Hanif's ambition illustrates:

I really wish I could find ways of being more imaginative without confusing the children... there's the desire to make the lesson more interesting.

He fully recognised the importance of presenting things clearly for a low-attaining group that tended to lose confidence very easily, but also appreciated that they would have welcomed something more light-hearted and fun, if only he had mastered a wider repertoire of strategies.

Another indication of the more aspirational end of the continuum is an increasing focus on classroom experimentation to develop both the trainee's learning and that of their pupils. Expressed in these ways, aspiration is strongly linked to intentionality – the capacity and commitment of the trainee to plan systematically for their own learning.

Intentionality

In characterising one end of this continuum as a *'reactive'* orientation, we are drawing on Eraut's definition of reactive learning as being *'near spontaneous and unplanned, the learner is aware of it but the level of intentionality will vary and often be debatable'*

(Eraut, 2000, p 115). Such an approach is perfectly epitomised in Rhiannon's claim that her learning was '*all just happening*' and only became evident to her when she looked back at her development. It is also reflected in Rob's rather defeatist vision of learning to teach as '*a never-ending tunnel*'. While many teachers positively declare (as Hanif did) that there is always more to be learned about teaching, Rob essentially interpreted this to mean that there is little point in striving too hard. A more reactive interpretation is therefore sometimes associated with trainees' abdication of responsibility for their own learning, or failure to consider how they might intervene in it. Rob recognised that he would probably benefit from more frequent observation and feedback, but exerted no effort to secure it.

Rob's response is in striking contrast to the efforts of another science trainee similarly frustrated by the limited feedback she was receiving as the year went on. She not only established a regular informal discussion meeting with other trainees and used this to launch a programme of shared observation and feedback, but she also made clear her interest in taking on more specific challenges:

I also feel that my learning is directed by me at this stage. I am the person saying "I'd like to teach more chemistry" or "I'd like to teach lower ability groups". I'm asking for more challenges.

This kind of proactive approach to creating opportunities for learning was typical of a '*deliberative*' orientation. Trainees with this approach could be seen formulating their next steps forward as part of the process of evaluating the lesson that they had just taught. Hanif, for example, peppered his review of a Year 12 lesson with decisions about what he needed to do before the next one, including practising the process of annotating a problem on the whiteboard as he worked through it so that he could model the process *live* with the students. A deliberative approach involves not just identifying the next target for development, but mapping out specific steps by which to tackle it. It also incorporates a conscious commitment to experimentation, conceived not as trial and error, but as deliberate testing of particular strategies. Among the DEBT trainees, it was exemplified by an English teacher who devoted the final weeks of her training to an action research project working with single-sex groups, and another science trainee who adopted a deliberate policy of using role-play to model particular chemical and biological processes.

While the contrast between trainees with proactive and reactive orientations might seem to suggest that the most important task for mentors is to keep providing feedback and establishing new targets, it is important to look beyond simply supplying your trainees with what they need next. The real challenge is to enable them to identify and begin to address those developmental needs *themselves*. In part this may depend on broadening their frame of reference – alerting them to the other resources on which they can draw.

Frame of reference

Within this dimension, the critical difference relates to the range of sources on which beginning teachers draw in making sense of their experience. At one end, it implies a narrow vision of reflective practice, based on simply looking in the mirror at one's own actions. On the other, it implies a much more expansive notion of reflection: critical examination of that practice from a range of different angles, illuminated by different sources. Among the DEBT trainees, these included: the advice and feedback offered by their mentor and other experienced teachers; observations of others' practice, schemes of work and teaching resources; wider reading (ranging from textbooks to academic scholarship within their subject, as well as educational research); and suggestions from their university-based tutors. While few specific instances of learning were directly attributed to such sources, the ways in which they were used both to generate and interpret particular experiences were very significant.

Because of the challenges of sustaining a dual role as teacher and learner, many trainees tend to restrict the sources on which they draw as the training year goes on. Sometimes they claim that *'shutting the classroom door'* is the only real way in which to make progress:

The need to be adaptable is coming through thick and fast now. You're going in and you're doing something. If it doesn't go to plan ... you've got to do something, rectify it and carry on. And I think that's something you could only learn from being on your own ... So that's the main way at the moment. Just being on your own and having to do it.

While the need to be adaptable and responsive is (as we have argued in Chapter 2) an essential characteristic of effective teaching, there is no reason why others cannot contribute to its development – not least by capturing examples of the trainees' interactions with pupils, allowing them to evaluate the impact of decisions taken in the heat of the moment.

A second, more nuanced, difference in the frames of reference on which trainees draw relates to the extent to which they recognise the *pupils* as sources from which they could learn. Here Rhiannon's practice in her training year contrasts sharply with that of Hanif. Early on, she saw pupils' diverse responses to particular tasks as a management problem. Thereafter she rarely mentioned them, except occasionally to comment on insights that she had gained from her marking. Hanif, on the other hand, was constantly alert to what the pupils' questions and answers (particularly the incorrect ones) revealed about their thinking and about the quality of his explanations.

Sometimes collecting data about the pupils' responses, rather than offering your own judgement on the quality of your trainees' teaching, may be one of the most useful contributions that you can make to their learning. It may also help to generate a more positive orientation towards feedback, especially if your trainee tends to take criticism personally.

Response to feedback

While the nature of your feedback on trainees' teaching and the way in which it is given will obviously impact on the way in which it is received, there are also marked differences in trainees' dispositions towards feedback, regardless of its quality. As Anita's story illustrates, some trainees have invested so much in teaching or are so desperate to prove their competence that they tend to be disabled by any kind of criticism and struggle to draw a distinction between judgements of their teaching and judgements of themselves. While Anita's vulnerability and sense that she had been judged a *'failure'* were particularly extreme, trainees who cannot separate the professional from the personal can easily feel overwhelmed by feedback intended to support them.

Others, in contrast, prove much more receptive to the comments made, recognising their ultimate focus on improving pupils' learning and seeking to understand how they should inform their subsequent planning. On occasion, trainees may even complain that the feedback they receive is not challenging enough. They are often much more critical of their own teaching than their mentor. Such self-deprecation (sometimes used as a form of self-defence when trainees are feeling vulnerable) is not necessarily a good thing either. As acknowledged earlier, perfectionism in a complex setting that demands judgement between competing priorities can be as unhelpful as limited ambition. What matters is the trainee's capacity to *make use* of the feedback (or of their own critique) to develop their practice. This may be determined in part by their attitude to the particular context in which they are placed.

Attitude to context

In considering the different orientations of beginning teachers towards the particular context in which they are gaining their experience, we define context quite broadly to include the nature of the school, the subject department, and the particular classes and pupils that they are teaching – as well as the role and status of the trainees themselves. The recent diversification of training routes means that there is now considerable variation in relation to the last of these factors. Mentors, used to working on one particular programme, who assume responsibilities for trainees on a different route, may need to think carefully about the implications of the change in terms of trainees' scope for action and sense of status. While some beginners may start their teaching effectively as guests in *'other people's classes'*, constrained by the regular teacher's expectations and routines, others have much more freedom but are held solely responsible for the pupils in their charge. Both contexts present different kinds of challenge and opportunity; but trainees can also react to the same context in different ways. While some complain, for example, that sharing classes makes it difficult to develop their own teaching style or to build relationships, others feel *'highly privileged'* to be working alongside experienced practitioners, and plan to exploit the scope that collaborative teaching gives them to experiment safely with more ambitious activities.

As these examples suggest, at one end of this dimension is a tendency for trainees to attribute blame for particular difficulties, or for their lack of progress, to particular features of the context. This orientation was occasionally displayed by Anita, as when she was obliged to begin teaching *'poems from other cultures'* but thought that the pupils deserved a more accessible or creative unit of study. Rather than embrace the challenge, seeing it as an opportunity to focus on making unfamiliar texts accessible, she effectively abdicated responsibility for the problems that arose, concluding that they were inevitable in the circumstances.

While Anita's sympathies essentially lay with the young people in her class, a tendency to attribute problems to the context can sometimes mean blaming the pupils. In one extreme case we encountered a science trainee so frustrated by the mismatch he perceived between the prescribed curriculum and the abilities of his class that all he could suggest doing was waiting until he was qualified, which would allow him to teach *'interesting things in a school where the academic standards are generally higher'*!

The opposite orientation is characterised by the trainee's acceptance of the context, notwithstanding the challenges that it presents, and a desire to exploit its particular features to promote their professional learning. Instead of becoming frustrated that teaching a certain group on Friday afternoon effectively rules out any prospect of developing productive group work, a trainee with a positive orientation to context might choose to focus instead on using pair work constructively. To do so would, of course, depend on the extent of the trainee's aspiration and their capacity to identify the first steps by which to work towards this – again revealing the interconnections between each of the different dimensions.

An emotional journey

So far this chapter has focused on two specific features of trainees' approach to the process of learning to teach: the ideas and assumptions about teaching and learning that they bring with them, and their orientations towards learning from experience. It has also called into question neatly ordered models of linear development. In this final section, we turn to a more universal psychological principle underpinning learning of any kind – the emotional state of the learner. Indeed it is, in part, the emotional component of each of those other elements that gives them such influence over trainees' development. Anita's vulnerability – the fact that feedback reduced her to tears – was rooted, in part, in her somewhat idealised view of teaching, as well as in her desperate desire to re-establish her sense of identity as a skilled and respected professional. Her high aspirations for pupils – the creative vision with which she wished to inspire them and the quality of the relationships that she intended to forge – made her early organisational failings particularly difficult to bear. Although she recognised at a rational level that the criticism that she was being given was 'very constructive', she still felt 'destroyed by it'. Her instincts were to run away: 'I don't want to go there. I feel like this child. I feel very vulnerable'.

While Anita's reaction was undoubtedly extreme, emotion played a powerful part in the trajectories of all our trainees. Even Hanif, a new graduate with much less at stake, who embraced teaching precisely because it would continually challenge and intrigue him, felt overwhelmed in early lessons by the catalogue of errors that he felt he had committed. His enthusiasm to list them for us – and, more importantly, to acknowledge them to his mentor – was partly an attempt to salvage some dignity, by demonstrating that he was well aware of them and knew what he needed to do to put them right next time. Although Rhiannon was less expressive of her emotions, the long-lasting constraints on her aspirations arose from her early loss of confidence. Her renewed curiosity two years later, as she began to explore how pupils made use of different strategies and recognised their capacity to surprise her, was extraordinarily uplifting. While Rob's sense of confidence undoubtedly made him somewhat complacent, it is worth noting the sense of stability and resilience that it also gave him – qualities that perhaps helped to sustain the quality of his teaching once he stopped receiving regular advice and feedback from his mentor.

The extent to which becoming a teacher is an 'affectively charged experience' (Hobson et al, 2008) is one of the most significant findings of the wide-ranging 'Becoming a Teacher' project which drew on a survey of nearly 4800 trainee teachers following different kinds of teacher preparation programmes, enriched by 85 in-depth interviews. The 'central *presence of emotion'* (Malderez et al, 2007, p 225) is one of four core features that the project revealed as fundamental to the process of becoming a trainee. Since *'teacher identity'* and the *'role of relationships'* constitute two of the others – and emotions play a vital part in both – it is not surprising that the research team urged training providers of all kinds to *'take more account of trainees' emotional states and welfare'* and to *'ensure that they provide effective support'* which helps them to *'navigate the inevitably emotionally charged process of becoming a teacher'* (Hobson et al, 2008, p 427).

Of course, not all of these emotions are negative. The joy of a breakthrough – when something *'clicks'* for a particular pupil, or when the effort invested in building a relationship with a *'difficult'* individual starts to pay off – can be truly exhilarating. But the fact that trainees are dealing with so many different pupils, each with particular needs, means that unequivocal success is rare. The sense that there is always more to improve makes it difficult for some trainees to acknowledge and celebrate the successes that they do achieve. The fact that so much of their affirmation comes from the relationships that they build with pupils means there is tremendous pressure to get them right. Yet beginning teachers are still trying to determine exactly what *right* means – struggling to work out how they can achieve their *'firm but fair'* or *'friendly but authoritative'* ideals.

It is not only relationships with pupils that matter profoundly. Trainees' relationships with colleagues, and particularly with their mentor, are extremely important too. But, again, such relationships are complicated, not least because of the dual roles that both you and they have to play. Your role as mentor usually combines advice and support with responsibility for assessment of the trainee. This can make the process of observation and feedback much more stressful for your trainee than you would wish. In their case the need to establish a new teacher identity, which means being seen as competent by others, can make the role of learner difficult to sustain. For those already aware of the mistakes that they have made in a particular lesson, the last thing they may need is to hear them enumerated by you. It is for these reasons that so many trainees can find themselves disabled by feedback genuinely intended to support them.

Acknowledging these complexities and realising how the *'emotional charge'* of learning to teach heightens the significance of your interactions with trainees may help you in making sensitive judgements about what is most appropriate to say at any given point, carefully calibrating what information your trainee needs and how it should be expressed so that they can use it productively.

IN A **NUTSHELL**

Long-standing theories of common stages in teacher development suggest that trainees move from an initial preoccupation with themselves (their own performance and developing sense of teacher identity) through a concern with managing and orchestrating the class to an eventual focus on the impact of their actions on pupils' learning. While there is some truth to this very broad pattern, it obscures the extent to which beginning teachers are wrestling with all these issues at once. Rather than assuming a series of sequential stages, it is much more helpful for mentors to focus on three significant facets of beginning teachers' learning and the interactions between them: the preconceptions that trainees bring with them; their particular orientations towards learning from experience; and the impact of their emotions on that process. While trainees' long *'apprenticeship of observation'* may give rise to an idealised vision of teaching, focused more on the quality of relationships than on understandings of pedagogy, it also inspires a passion for pupils' learning that can be acknowledged and cultivated from the start of the training year. But if those high aspirations are not underpinned by a deliberative approach towards learning from experience – conscious planning of the steps by which they can gradually be achieved – they may lead quickly to despair. Your support in calibrating those steps, and thus ensuring that the trainees' ambitions and sense of professional competence are reinforced by early successes, makes it much more likely that the emotional feedback loop, which impacts so powerfully on most trainees, will work positively rather than negatively.

REFLECTIONS ON **CRITICAL ISSUES**

- *Beginning teachers embark on their training with a number of deep-seated preconceptions, derived from their own experience as pupils and often from previous teaching roles. Since these preconceptions may give rise to idealised visions and simplistic assumptions about the ease of learning from experience, it is important that they are acknowledged and critically examined.*
- *Some common patterns can be discerned in beginning teachers' development, such as a shift from 'early idealism' to a 'struggle for survival' as they seek to master the complexities of managing both the class and the learning activities they have planned. However, such systematic models mask both the extent of individual variation and the fact that beginners do not deal with different issues in a neat, sequential fashion.*
- *While all beginning teachers rightly expect to learn from experience, the ways in which they engage in that process vary significantly in relation to five inter-related dimensions: the extent of their aspirations; the degree of intentionality in planning for their own learning; the frame of reference on which they draw in making sense of experience; their response to feedback; and their attitude to the context in which they are placed.*
- *The challenges of establishing a new teacher identity and building productive relationships with both pupils and colleagues make learning to teach an emotionally charged process, in which perceptions of success and failure are powerfully amplified. It is essential to acknowledge this vulnerability in judging how to present advice and feedback.*

CHAPTER 4

HOW CAN WE HELP BEGINNING TEACHERS TO BECOME MORE EFFECTIVE LEARNERS?

CRITICAL **ISSUES**

- *How can you, as a mentor, help your trainees to articulate their preconceptions and so acknowledge their influence and begin to subject them to critical scrutiny?*
- *How can you construct an appropriate curriculum for your trainees' learning, given that the competing demands of teaching are encountered simultaneously and not in a carefully staged sequence?*
- *How can you help your trainees to embrace and sustain a dual identity as both teacher and learner, thereby establishing a sustainable commitment to continued professional learning?*
- *How can you encourage your trainees to adopt a more deliberative approach towards their own learning, enabling them to take increasing responsibility for directing their own development?*
- *How can you expand the frame of reference on which your trainees draw in making sense of their experience, equipping them to learn effectively from the wealth of resources available to them within school and beyond?*

Eliciting trainees' preconceptions

Our central argument is that it is only by paying serious attention to the nature of teaching itself and to the ways in which beginning teachers engage in the process of learning to teach that you can help them to capitalise on the main source from which they expect to learn – their classroom experience. This final chapter addresses the challenge of *making experience count* by setting out five principles for supporting trainees' learning that fully acknowledge both the demands of learning to teach (as explained in Chapter 2) and all that we have learned about beginning teachers as learners (Chapter 3).

The most logical place to start, because of the power that they exercise over beginning teachers' development, is with the preconceptions that trainees bring with them. Eliciting those preconceptions is an essential first step in enabling your trainee to acknowledge their influence and so begin to subject them to critical scrutiny.

Beginning teachers, as they embark on their training, *'are no more empty vessels than are children as they enter classrooms'* (Hagger and McIntyre, 2006, p 42). Your trainee's prior experiences not only provide them with models of teaching to which they aspire (or perhaps emphatically reject) but also shape the lens through which they view their subsequent experience and the practical advice that you offer them. Taking time early on to ask about those previous experiences and sources of inspiration will give you important insights into some of the views that your trainee holds about teaching and learning, and into the contexts in which they were developed. Understanding those roots will help you both to appreciate the emotional attachment that your trainee might have to those ideas and enable you to support them in evaluating their relevance and meaning in their current context.

When beginning teachers first arrive in school, it is easy to focus exclusively on all the things that they will need to know in order to function effectively. In planning for a trainee induction programme you are likely to find the introduction of essential policies and procedures vying for attention with details of the curriculum and exam specifications, along with more urgent practical issues, such as the basic geography of the school, introductions to key personnel and access to essential IT systems. Overwhelmed by the information that you have to impart, it can be difficult to recognise the importance of also asking questions. But time devoted to establishing where each particular trainee is coming from – seeking out their impressions of their own school experience, inviting recollections of the teachers that they wish to emulate and those that epitomise all that they want to avoid – not only communicates your interest in each of them as an individual (an essential first step in reassuring them of your support), but also provides you with vital points of reference. Later, being able to link the advice that you give to images that they already hold, or to explicitly acknowledge that what you are suggesting might seem counter-intuitive in light of their ideals, means that you will be able to help your trainee to connect those new insights to their existing ideas, thereby engaging their *'initial understanding'* (Donovan and Bransford, 2005, p 1), which makes the prospect of critical evaluation and subsequent development much more likely.

Getting into the habit of asking questions of your trainee rather than simply telling them what you think they ought to know is an invaluable strategy to adopt throughout the training year. Just as effective questioning serves as an essential tool of formative assessment (Black et al, 2002) because of the way in which it reveals pupils' current understanding and ways of thinking, so it can help you to determine the kinds of advice or feedback that may be most useful to your trainee at any particular point. It will also help you to decide how best to structure the trainee's curriculum, determining the particular balance of their timetable at various stages or the kinds of activity in which it might be most useful for them to engage.

Structuring trainees' access to the curriculum of initial teacher education

The question of how to construct an appropriate curriculum lies at the heart of the challenge of making experience count. The very fact that trainees need to learn to draw flexibly on a wide range of knowledge bases as they confront the *'multidimensionality'* and *'unpredictability'* (Doyle, 1977) of the classroom seems to make a mockery of any attempt to structure that learning into a coherent programme – even before you acknowledge that beginners do not all follow neatly ordered trajectories, dealing first with classroom management and the organisation of tasks and then with pupils' learning. When both facts are considered together, it becomes obvious that, while you certainly want to avoid your trainees feeling overwhelmed by all that they need to learn, the very nature of what they are trying to learn means that it cannot be neatly packaged for them in a series of discrete units. Attempting to do so would not only divert you from the reality of your trainees' current priorities, it would also represent a scandalous waste of the potential of school-based teacher education. As Hagger and McIntyre argue, the whole point of work-based learning is that the learning is about the realities of the work.

It is of the greatest importance that the normal realities of how work is organized and of how people do their work should not be distorted by the ways in which learning tasks are structured... [W]ork-based learning needs to be structured as much as is necessary to maximize learners' cognitive access to the full normal realities of doing the work, but must not distort these realities.

(Hagger and McIntyre, 2006, pp 49–50)

In thinking about how to structure trainees' learning in school, it quickly becomes clear that most of the curriculum that they need is, in fact, already laid out in the realities of teachers' practice and pupils' learning, as they happen in classrooms. Our second principle is therefore framed not as a process of constructing a curriculum for trainees' school-based learning but as one of organising or structuring trainees' *access* to that curriculum. While observation and learning by doing both have a critical role to play, neither of them, as we have shown, is straightforward or guaranteed to prove effective: prior experience as a pupil can obscure rather than help beginners to interpret experienced teachers' classroom decision-making; simple imitation of others' practice will never give rise to the *'adaptive expertise'* (Hammerness et al, 2005) that teachers actually need.

So, if trainees need to encounter teaching as it actually is, and if their own preconceptions and particular agendas play a powerful role in determining what they will attend to within those encounters, what processes can be used to maximise the learning opportunities that they present?

A learning timetable – not simply a teaching schedule

The first process is careful design of your trainee's timetable. Although different training routes will inevitably have different implications for the kind of teaching responsibilities assigned to trainees, it is essential to ensure that every trainee has sufficient time both to plan for and to review their early teaching experiences. Planning, especially in the beginning, when trainees' knowledge is likely to be limited in relation to all of the essential bases (except, perhaps, subject matter), is intensely time-consuming. Working from existing schemes of work or lesson plans devised by experienced teachers does not necessarily speed things up, since it still involves the trainee in a process of interpretation and reconstruction in light of their own understanding of the underlying objectives and their own restricted repertoire of teaching strategies. Post-lesson reflection also takes time – and the capacity to focus. Without the opportunity to look in detail at specific aspects of what happened, it is easy for trainees to make sweeping judgements (heavily skewed by their own emotional state), drawing on limited evidence. If trainees feel under constant pressure to get on with planning the next lesson, they are unlikely to devote the necessary time to unpacking and reviewing different phases of the previous one, or to examining particular decisions that they took and the pupils' responses to them.

To ensure that beginners get the time that they need, particularly in the early stages, it makes sense to give them a carefully protected introduction, building their teaching commitments slowly so that they do not outstrip their capacity to learn effectively from them. Even if you have no scope to give your trainee a phased introduction to their timetable, you may still be able to influence the range of classes assigned to them, thereby reducing some of the planning demands and facilitating more effective reflection. At secondary level, for example, teaching two or more parallel classes within the same year group gives trainees the opportunity to evaluate and adapt each lesson in light of the pupils' responses before teaching it again.

Engagement in collaborative planning and teaching

One way of easing the demands of planning, early on, is for you and your trainee to plan together. This would also require you to articulate both the processes in which you engage as you plan and the professional knowledge that informs them, making explicit to your trainee the wide range of considerations that shape your decision-making. While this is obviously a time-consuming process, it is a much more productive use of time than asking novices to plan lessons unaided, then delivering a critique of their proposals and expecting them to be revised. Calling for extensive adaptations after a trainee has invested considerable time and effort in the first draft can be both soul-destroying and panic-inducing, especially if there is little time left before the lesson to make the necessary changes.

Working collaboratively instead, as Burn (1997) has demonstrated, gives beginners access to experienced teachers' methods and insights in a variety of different ways. These include mentors modelling the sequence of their planning, for example, by working back from the desired outcome or learning objective to determine the route by which it could be achieved (rather than starting, as many beginners do, with an idea for a good activity); mentors visualising likely pupil responses to a particular question or task as a means of assessing its value and feasibility; and mentors exemplifying the ways in which they transform their subject knowledge into a simplified form for pupils.

Where timetables permit, collaborative teaching also allows the trainee to take responsibility for specifically chosen parts of a lesson, coming to terms with real teaching while remaining in a protected environment.

By narrowing the focus and removing some of the panic and confusion, it allows [trainees] to approach the task of teaching more rationally, both while engaged in teaching and in analysing it afterwards.

(Burn, 1997, p 160)

Although such collaboration takes considerable time, investment in it at the start of the training year will enable you and your trainee to develop a shared body of knowledge and understanding that can be increasingly taken for granted, allowing you then to focus on particular development priorities and on the use of more imaginative or demanding teaching strategies. You can, of course, also adapt the scale, moving from planning single lessons to extended teaching sequences and schemes of work, thereby modelling and inducting the trainee into the process of curriculum development within your year or subject team.

Careful progression in lesson feedback and evaluation

Formative evaluation of trainees' teaching – the process of observation and feedback – is the most obvious process through which you can effectively structure beginners' access to all that can be learned from the realities of teaching. The fact that you are focusing on their classroom experience – the very source from which trainees expect to learn most – gives you unparalleled scope to articulate your own craft knowledge in relevant and comprehensible ways that engage directly with their current agenda.

However, while collaborative planning allows you to work *alongside* your trainee, the process of giving feedback tends to foreground the hierarchical nature of your relationship and alert the trainee to the role that you play in assessment of their eventual competence. These unspoken assumptions, combined with the trainees' anxiety to demonstrate their proficiency and so lay claim to a new teacher identity, also increase the potential for it to be one of the most emotionally charged processes in learning to teach.

This charge can be defused in two important ways. The first is by encouraging the trainee to offer their reflections first, which allows you to tune into *their* agenda and to take stock of their emotional state. It also alerts you to the thinking that informed their decisions, helping you to judge whether particular difficulties derive from unhelpful or unproductive ideas per se, or simply from a current inability to execute appropriate strategies effectively. You can then decide not only what feedback is actually necessary (in many cases trainees, like Hanif, will anticipate the very judgements that you had intended to make), but also what might be most important, and most helpful, to share. While this will be determined in part by your judgement of the pupils' most urgent needs, it will also take account of the trainee's sense of priorities, engaging, where possible, with them (since these are the issues to which they are most likely to attend), or at least ensuring that you explain clearly why you regard other issues as more important.

The second way of defusing the emotional charge associated with feedback is by ensuring that the trainee's reflections – and your own – focus first on aspects of strength, identifying what went well and seeking to establish the reasons why. Only when you and they have acknowledged a number of specific aspects for which they should take credit, and established what can be learned from them, should you allow the trainee to focus on those aspects which they know need further development. Trainees' resilience and capacity to go on learning are sustained as much by experiences of success as by the quality of the suggestions that you give them about how they could improve their practice.

None of this is to suggest that you *only* follow their agenda. Obviously, the award of qualified teacher status depends on the achievement of defined standards, and you need to ensure that, over time, these are all addressed. Similarly, you need to ensure that trainees' knowledge and understanding are being developed in relation to all of the knowledge bases enumerated in Chapter 2, with due acknowledgement of the interplay between them. But by encouraging the trainee to assume responsibility for leading the evaluation of their teaching, identifying the areas of strength and targets for development (and the evidence on which they are basing these judgements) *before* they have heard your views, you are also promoting the development of a more deliberative orientation towards their own learning. Their continued professional development will depend on the extent to which they have internalised this habit of forward planning, informed by careful evaluation.

Focused observation of experienced teachers' practice

While we have argued for a phased introduction to trainees' teaching, where possible, we do not mean that they should begin with a diet of lesson observation, gradually supplemented by collaborative teaching and then slowly replaced by solo teaching opportunities. While some trainees, particularly those who have been away from the classroom for some time, may welcome a period of familiarisation, most find it difficult to learn productively from simple observation of experienced teachers and are anxious to abandon the practice as quickly as possible. Engaging in extensive observation early on tends to inoculate trainees against its subsequent benefits!

As Hagger (1997) and Hagger and McIntyre (2006) have demonstrated, observation becomes a much more productive process of learning later in the year, when beginners are more aware of the complexity of teaching and can appreciate the diverse needs of individual learners and the competing objectives that teachers may be seeking to prioritise. Using focused observation at this point, particularly in conjunction with planned opportunities to discuss the lesson afterwards with the teacher concerned, asking non-judgemental questions about the reasons for their decisions and their reaction to the outcomes, offers a tremendous insight into the process of clinical reasoning – the *'analytical and intuitive cognitive processes that professionals use to arrive at a best judged ethical response in a specific practice-based context'* (Kriewaldt and Turnidge, 2013, p 106) – as it actually operates in experienced teachers' thinking.

Consulting pupils about their experience of learning

One other process by which trainees can be helped to subject the messy realities of teaching to rational analysis is by seeking feedback from pupils about their experiences of learning. Obviously, pupils' oral responses in lessons and the dialogue that occurs between pupil and teacher as part of the marking and feedback process both provide some insight into pupils' perspectives. This can be significantly enriched, however, by seeking specific feedback on the pupils' experience of different kinds of learning task, the ease or difficulty with which they tackled it, and how helpful they found both the activity and the associated teacher explanations and guidance. This is obviously a risky strategy, since it might appear to cast the pupils as a panel of judges assessing the quality of the trainee's performance, thereby triggering excessive anxiety. However, as Rudduck and McIntyre (2007) have shown, pupils are not merely highly knowledgeable informants, they also tend to respond thoughtfully and sensitively when they recognise that their views are genuinely valued. Obviously, the questions that they are asked need to be carefully planned, so that the focus is on their experience and sense of their own understanding rather than on the trainee's performance, but it certainly does not need to be onerous. One or two questions answered on a sticky note at the end of a lesson, especially when considered alongside the pupils' written work, may prove invaluable, alerting a trainee to particular kinds of misconception or to the kinds of strategy that the pupils found most helpful in moving them forward.

Sustaining the trainee's dual identity as teacher and learner

Of course, consulting pupils about their learning is only likely to be embraced by trainees if they think that experienced teachers also regard it as an important source for their own learning. If pupils' views are not valued by qualified practitioners, then trainees, anxious to establish their professional credibility, are unlikely to want to distinguish themselves as novices by drawing pupils' attention to their interest in learning from them. This focuses attention on the third essential principle that should guide your practice in making trainees' experience count: sustaining your trainee's dual identity as both teacher and learner.

The most effective way of doing this, as we have already suggested, is by demonstrating your own commitment to continued professional learning, embodying precisely those orientations towards learning from experience that play such a crucial role in trainees' development. If trainees can see that you recognise the pupils as a key resource for developing your practice and that you seek their opinions in evaluating particular innovations, they are much more likely to adopt such approaches as part of their own professional repertoire. If they are aware not just of your own professional development priorities but also of the first steps that you have identified in working towards their achievement, trainees are much more likely to regard the process of target-setting not simply as a requirement of their training programme but as an essential component of a deliberative approach to future development.

It is important not to underestimate the impact that your example can have on your trainees, but obviously this kind of modelling will be even more effective if beginners encounter it throughout the school. In such circumstances the benefits are likely to be widely apparent – given the weight of national and international evidence (BERA-RSA, 2014) pointing to the impact of enquiry-based or research-rich environments in which teachers are committed not only to keeping up to date with the latest developments (in their subject domains as well as within education research) but also to engaging in enquiry-oriented practice. While recent reports (BERA-RSA, 2014; Carter, 2015) have called for these habits to be established within initial teacher education, the process is a reciprocal one, with novices more likely to develop those professional habits that their experienced colleagues clearly value.

Promoting a deliberative approach towards learning from experience

The notion of *engaging in enquiry-oriented practice* is essentially an extension of what we have described among beginners as a deliberative orientation towards learning from experience. *Enquiry* is perhaps more open-ended than *deliberation,* suggesting a greater sense of curiosity, with teachers consciously asking questions about aspects of practice or pupils' experience. But both terms imply an explicit commitment to the process of continuing professional development, and to the kinds of action necessary to bring this about. The process may not be as extensive or rigorous as action research but it certainly requires deliberate planning; determining a clear focus for improvement; investigating and reflecting on what is revealed about current realities; and then adapting practice in light of the findings (and perhaps on the basis of evidence or advice from other sources) before collecting further evidence to review the impact of the modifications. As with the specific process of seeking feedback from pupils, the more that trainees see their mentors engaged in this kind of deliberative practice, the more likely they are to recognise its value. This relates directly to our fourth principle – that of promoting a deliberative orientation towards learning from experience.

Modelling such a deliberative orientation yourself and alerting your trainees to ways in which it may be embodied in specific professional development initiatives within your school (such as lesson study, action learning sets or professional learning communities) offers one way of promoting it. Another highly effective strategy, as we have noted, is that of inviting your trainees to contribute *first* whenever you are giving feedback on their teaching. Adopting this strategy from the very beginning and persisting with it, even if your trainees find it difficult at first, makes it much more likely that they will recognise and embrace the responsibility that they have to make their own judgements and to identify the implications of those judgements for their future development – rather than simply relying on you for affirmation and direction. As we have pointed out, inviting the trainee to present their own views first certainly does not mean that you refrain from any kind of evaluation or from offering specific advice. The explanations that you propose for what happened and your suggestions about possible ways forward are invaluable in making your expertise available to beginners. But by expecting them to put forward their own views (with an explanation of the evidence on which they are based) and to make specific suggestions about how they intend to respond to what they have learned, you are much more likely to establish the principle that professional responsibility ultimately will lie with them and to ensure that their aspirations are consistently supported by specific steps forward.

You can also support this forward movement by ensuring that any discussion of observed teaching concludes not simply with a number of points for future development but with the identification of particular ways in which the trainee can begin to address them. Rather than merely noting, for example, a need to *'improve the use of questioning'*, it is important both to identify the specific characteristics that they should be seeking to develop – such as the involvement of a wider range of pupils or more systematic encouragement for them to explain the thinking behind their answer – and suggestions as to how the trainee might learn to develop these particular features within their practice. These might include:

» focused observation of an experienced teacher, known to be particularly skilled in this respect;

» deliberate experimentation with particular strategies, perhaps originally derived from research – such as the use of named lolly-sticks drawn at random, or a *'think, pair, share'* process by which pupils are given dedicated thinking time and the opportunity to discuss their initial ideas with a partner before being expected to respond;

» advance planning of some of the specific questions that they intend to ask, rehearsing their actual phrasing and generating a list of possible prompts to elicit further explanation;

» identification on their lesson plan of specific students to whom particular questions should first be directed;

» video- or audio-recording of their own teaching, enabling them to replay and analyse the phrasing of their questions and the time that they allowed for pupils to formulate their response.

This range of suggestions – some of which are clearly focused within the trainee's own classroom while others direct them to look beyond it – serve to demonstrate the importance of our final principle: expanding the frame of reference on which trainees draw.

Expanding trainees' frames of reference

Expansion, as we have suggested, needs to happen in both directions: reaching deep *within* the trainees' class to ensure that they recognise the range of insights that they can gain from the pupils themselves, as well as looking *beyond* that particular context to draw on ideas and practices developed and refined by experienced colleagues or more systematically analysed and evaluated through different kinds of research. While you have a crucial role to play in facilitating trainees' access to the range of sources available to them in school, again your most important contribution probably derives from the way in which you model an open-minded and enquiring disposition.

Assuming the role of mentor should not mean that your practice becomes the standard frame of reference for your trainees. While it might be helpful for you to work very closely with them in the early stages, it is much more productive to think of mentoring as the responsibility of a whole subject department (in secondary schools) or of a year or key-stage team (in primary settings). Your oversight of the trainee's learning means that you can identify colleagues who may be particularly able to help with specific developmental needs, but observing and asking questions of a range of different teachers will also give your trainee a much more developed appreciation of the role of interpretation and judgement in teachers' decision-making.

Most training programmes are offered in the context of some kind of partnership, linking schools to one another and/or connecting them with university providers. This obviously provides trainees with access to wider sources of learning. Particular course demands – most obviously formal assignments – may also oblige them to engage in particular kinds of reading or systematic investigation of specific issues. Although these demands can sometimes be seen as distractions from the *real* business of teaching, the way in which *you* respond to them is crucial in ensuring that those wider sources of learning are actually brought to bear on the real issues that confront your trainees. If those issues are also of concern to you and to your colleagues, there is real scope for you to learn together by encouraging the trainee to share what they are reading, or to feedback to the whole department or year team on the findings of their investigation. If the trainee is allowed to choose the focus of their assignment, you might offer them specific suggestions, linked to department or school development priorities. Seeing those connections and the value of the work to you is likely to enhance its value to the trainee.

IN A **NUTSHELL**

Our first draft of this chapter included one more question, arising particularly from what we know about beginning teachers as learners, asking how mentors could best take account of the emotionally charged nature of learning to teach. The power of trainees' emotions, as they seek to establish a new professional identity and build the relationships with pupils and colleagues that are so fundamental to effective teaching, makes this one of the most important questions of all. But as we drafted the five principles presented here – principles intended to ensure that your trainee's experience really does count – we realised that in enacting them, you would be taking effective account of the emotionally charged nature of trainees' learning, minimising its destructive tendencies and establishing a positive feedback loop. Taking time to find out about, and showing that you value and acknowledge, the influence of their prior experiences is an important foundation for a genuine relationship with your trainee. Designing a learning timetable responsive to their particular needs rather than imposing a teaching schedule upon them will help to ensure that they are not initially overwhelmed. Demonstrating by your own example that experienced teachers are still engaged in learning and modelling for your trainee the continued excitement to be found in new discoveries and effective refinements of practice will make them feel less anxious about the dual identity that they are required to sustain. Promoting a deliberative orientation by first inviting your trainee to share their own perceptions of an observed lesson will gradually make them less anxious about your judgements of them, ensuring that they have formulated a series of steps by which to target those aspects in need of development will give them a much greater sense of agency. So, too, will your reminders of all the other sources of support and guidance on which they can draw – especially if you also welcome and engage with the insights that they gain from them.

REFLECTIONS ON **CRITICAL ISSUES**

- *The most effective way of eliciting trainees' preconceptions is by making time when they first join the school to talk to them about their experience as a pupil and about any previous teaching roles (formal or informal) that they may have held. Sustain that habit of asking questions first, seeking to understand how your trainee sees things before offering your own analysis and advice.*

- *Since the curriculum that your trainees need to master is presented to them in the realities of classroom practice, you cannot map out a series of discrete topics for them to follow. You need to concentrate instead on the processes by which you can structure their access to that curriculum, through the construction of a learning timetable (not a teaching schedule), enagement in collaborative planning, careful progression in lesson evaluation and feedback, focused observation of experienced teachers' practice, and consultation with pupils about their experience of learning.*

- *The most effective way of sustaining your trainee's dual identity as both teacher and learner is by embracing both roles yourself, clearly demonstrating the importance of continued learning as intrinsic to your professional identity as a teacher.*

- *Modelling a deliberative approach to your own learning from experience will also serve to promote that kind of orientation in your trainee. You can support the development of such an approach from the very beginning by ensuring that the trainee shares their perceptions of an observed lesson before seeking your opinions and that any aspects for development that are identified are accompanied by specific steps forward which will expand their knowledge and understanding, and promote changes in practice. As time goes on, you can extend the same model of forward planning beyond immediate priorities to engage and build on their long-term aspirations.*

- *You can expand trainees' frame of refence within and beyond their classroom, by encouraging them to focus in-depth on their pupils' experiences of learning; by extending the reponsibility for mentoring beyond you to your department or year team; and by inviting trainees to share with you and your colleagues what they are learning from their reading of research or professional literaure and from their more formal investigations of practice.*

REFERENCES

Ball, S (2003) The Teacher's Soul and the Terrors of Performativity. *Journal of Education Policy*, 18(2): 215–28.

BERA-RSA (2014) *Research and the Teaching Profession Building the Capacity for a Self-Improving Education System*. London: British Education Research Association.

Black, P and Wiliam, D (1998) *Inside the Black Box*. London: King's College.

Black, P, Harrison, C, Lee, C, Marshall, B and Wiliam, D (2002) *Working Inside the Black Box: Assessment for Learning in the Classroom*. London: King's College.

Black, P, Harrison, C, Lee, C, Marshall, B and Wiliam, D (2003) *Assessment for Learning: Putting It into Practice*. Maidenhead: Open University Press.

Bransford, J, Darling-Hammond, L and LePage, P (2005) Introduction, in Darling-Hammond, L, Bransford, J, LePage, P, Hammerness, K and Duffy, H (eds) *Preparing Teachers for a Changing World: What Teachers Should Learn and Be Able to Do*. San Francisco: Jossey-Bass.

Buchmann, M (1984) The Priority of Knowledge and Understanding in Teaching, in Katz, L and Raths, J (eds) *Advances in Teacher Education, Vol. 1*. Norwood, NJ: Abley.

Bullough, R (Jr), Young, J and Draper, R (2004) One-year Teaching Internships and the Dimensions of Beginning Teacher Development. *Teachers and Teaching: Theory and Practice* 10(4): 365–94.

Burn, K (1997) Learning to Teach: The Value of Collaborative Teaching, in McIntyre, D (ed) *Teacher Education Research in a New Context: The Oxford Internship Scheme*. London: Paul Chapman.

Burn, K, Hagger, H and Mutton, T (2010) Strengthening and Sustaining Learning in the Second Year of Teaching. *Oxford Review of Education*, 36(6): 639–59.

Burn, K, Hagger, H, Mutton, T and Everton, T (2000) Beyond Concerns with Self: The Sophisticated Thinking of Beginning Student Teachers. *Journal of Education for Teaching*, 26(3): 259–78.

Burn, K, Hagger, H, Mutton, T and Everton, T (2003) The Complex Development of Student-Teachers' Thinking. *Teachers and Teaching: Theory and Practice*, 9(4): 309–21.

Carter, A (2015) *Carter Review of Initial Teacher Training (ITT)*. London: Department for Education.

Conway, P and Clark, C (2003) The Journey Inward and Outward: A Re-Examination of Fuller's Concerns-Based Model of Teacher Development. *Teaching and Teacher Education* 19(5): 465–82.

Darling-Hammond, L (2006) Constructing 21st-Century Teacher Education. *Journal of Teacher Education*, 57(3): 300–14.

Donovan, M and Bransford, J (eds) (2005) *How Students Learn: History, Mathematics, and Science in the Classroom*. Washington, DC: National Academy of Sciences.

Doyle, W (1977) Learning the Classroom Environment: An Ecological Analysis. *Journal of Teacher Education*, 28(6): 51–5.

Eraut, M (1994) *Developing Professional Knowledge and Competence*. London: Falmer.

Eraut, M (2000) Non-Formal Learning and Tacit Knowledge in Professional Work. *British Journal of Educational Psychology*, 70(1): 113–36.

Fuller, F and Bown, O (1975) Becoming a Teacher, in Ryan, K (ed) *Teacher Education: The Seventy-Fourth Yearbook of the National Society for the Study of Education*. Chicago, IL: University of Chicago Press.

Furlong, J and Maynard, T (1995) *Mentoring Student Teachers: The Growth of Professional Knowledge*. London: Routledge.

Guillaume, A and Rudney, G (1993) Student Teachers' Growth Toward Independence: An Analysis of Their Changing Concerns. *Teaching and Teacher Education*, 9(1): 65–80.

Hagger, H (1997) Enabling Student Teachers to Gain Access to the Professional Craft Knowledge of Experienced Teachers, in McIntyre, D (ed) *Teacher Education Research in a New Context: The Oxford Internship Scheme*. London: Paul Chapman Publishing.

Hagger, H, Burn, K and McIntyre, D (1993) *The School Mentor Handbook: Essential Skills and Strategies for Working with Student Teachers*. London: Kogan Page.

Hagger, H, Burn, K, Mutton, T and Brindley, S (2008) Practice Makes Perfect? Learning to Learn as a Teacher. *Oxford Review of Education*, 34(2): 159–78.

Hagger, H and McIntyre, D (2006) *Learning Teaching from Teachers: Realizing the Potential of School-Based Teacher Education*. Maidenhead: Open University Press.

Hammerness, K, Darling-Hammond, L and Bransford, J with Berliner, D, Cochran-Smith, M, McDonald, M and Zeichner, K (2005) How Teachers Learn and Develop, in Darling-Hammond, L and Bransford, J with LePage, P, Hammerness, K and Duffy, H (eds) *Preparing Teachers for a Changing World: What Teachers Should Learn and Be Able to Do*. San Francisco: Jossey-Bass.

Hargreaves, D, Dowitch, M and Giffin, D (1997) *On-the-Job Training for Surgeons*. London: Royal Society of Medicine Press.

Hobson, A, Malderez, A, Tracey, L, Giannakaki, M, Pell, G and Tomlinson, P (2008) Student Teachers' Experiences of Initial Teacher Preparation in England: Core Themes and Variation. *Research Papers in Education*, 23(4): 407–33.

Kennedy, M (2006) Knowledge and Vision in Teaching. *Journal of Teacher Education*, 57(3): 205–11.

Kriewaldt, J and Turnidge, D (2013) Conceptualising an Approach to Clinical Reasoning in the Education Profession. *Australian Journal of Teacher Education*, 38(6): 102–15.

Lacey, C (1977) *The Socialization of Teachers*. London: Methuen.

Lortie, D C (1975) *Schoolteacher: A Sociological Study*. Chicago: University of Chicago Press.

Malderez, A, Hobson, A, Tracey, L and Kerr, K (2007) Becoming a Student Teacher: Core Features of the Experience. *European Journal of Teacher Education*, 30(3): 225–48.

Mattsson, M, Eilertson, T and Rorrison, D (eds) (2011) *A Practicum Turn in Teacher Education*. Rotterdam: Sense.

Mutton, T, Burn, K and Hagger, H (2010) Making Sense of Learning to Teach: Learners in Context. *Research Papers in Education*, 25(1): 73–91.

Mutton, T, Hagger, H and Burn, K (2011) Learning to Plan, Planning to Learn: The Developing Expertise of Beginning Teachers. *Teachers and Teaching: Theory and Practice*, 17(4): 399–416.

Pendry, A (1997) The Pedagogical Thinking and Learning of History Teachers, in McIntyre, D (ed) *Teacher Education Research in a New Context: The Oxford Internship Scheme*. London: Paul Chapman Publishing.

Pillen, M, Beijaard, D and Den Brok, P (2013) Tensions in Beginning Teachers' Professional Identity Development, Accompanying Feelings and Coping Strategies. *European Journal of Teacher Education*, 36(3): 240–60.

Rice, K G and Lapsley, D K (2001) Perfectionism, Coping, and Emotional Adjustment. *Journal of College Student Development* 42(2): 157–68.

Rudduck, J and McIntyre, D (2007) *Improving Learning through Consulting Pupils*. London: Routledge.

Shulman, L (1986) Those Who Understand: Knowledge Growth in Teaching. *Educational Researcher*, 15(2): 4–14.

Shulman, L (1998) Theory, Practice and the Education of Professionals. *The Elementary School Journal* 98(5): 511–26.

Watzke, J (2007) Longitudinal Research on Beginning Teacher Development: Complexity as a Challenge to Concerns-Based Stage Theory. *Teaching and Teacher Education* 23(1):106–22.

Younger, M, Brindley, S, Pedder, D and Hagger, H (2004) Starting Points: Student Teachers' Reasons for Becoming Teachers and Their Preconceptions of What This Will Mean. *European Journal of Teacher Education*, 27(3): 245–64.

Zeichner, K (1996) Designing Educative Practicum Experiences, in Zeichner, K, Melnick, S and Gomez, M L (eds) *Currents of Reform in Preservice Teacher Education*. New York: Teachers College Press.

INDEX